The First Men

LIFE WORLD LIBRARY
LIFE NATURE LIBRARY
TIME READING PROGRAM
THE LIFE HISTORY OF THE UNITED STATES
LIFE SCIENCE LIBRARY
GREAT AGES OF MAN
TIME-LIFE LIBRARY OF ART
TIME-LIFE LIBRARY OF AMERICA
FOODS OF THE WORLD
THIS FABULOUS CENTURY
LIFE LIBRARY OF PHOTOGRAPHY
THE TIME-LIFE ENCYCLOPEDIA OF GARDENING
THE AMERICAN WILDERNESS
THE EMERGENCE OF MAN
THE OLD WEST
FAMILY LIBRARY:
  THE TIME-LIFE BOOK OF FAMILY FINANCE
  THE TIME-LIFE FAMILY LEGAL GUIDE

The Emergence of Man

The First Men

by the Editors
of TIME-LIFE BOOKS

TIME-LIFE BOOKS
New York

TIME-LIFE BOOKS

FOUNDER: Henry R. Luce 1898-1967

Editor-in-Chief: Hedley Donovan
Chairman of the Board: Andrew Heiskell
President: James R. Shepley
Chairman, Executive Committee: James A. Linen
Editorial Director: Louis Banks
Group Vice President: Rhett Austell

Vice Chairman: Roy E. Larsen

EDITOR: Jerry Korn
Executive Editor: A. B. C. Whipple
Planning Director: Oliver E. Allen
Text Director: Martin Mann
Art Director: Sheldon Cotler
Chief of Research: Beatrice T. Dobie
Director of Photography: Melvin L. Scott
Assistant Text Directors:
Ogden Tanner, Diana Hirsh
Assistant Art Director: Arnold C. Holeywell

PUBLISHER: Joan D. Manley
General Manager: John D. McSweeney
Business Manager: John Steven Maxwell
Sales Director: Carl G. Jaeger
Promotion Director: Paul R. Stewart
Public Relations Director: Nicholas Benton

THE EMERGENCE OF MAN
SERIES EDITOR: Carlotta Kerwin
Editorial Staff for *The First Men:*
Text Editor: Harvey B. Loomis
Picture Editors: Edward Brash, Jane Scholl
Designer: William Rose
Staff Writers: Helen Barer, Suzanne Seixas
Chief Researcher: David L. Harrison
Researchers: Muriel B. Clarke, Helen Greenway,
Brenda Huff, Kumait Jawdat,
Susan Jonas, Diana Sweeney
Design Assistant: Lee Wilfert

Editorial Production
Production Editor: Douglas B. Graham
Quality Director: Robert L. Young
Assistant: James J. Cox
Copy Staff: Rosalind Stubenberg,
Susan B. Galloway, Florence Keith
Picture Department: Dolores A. Littles, Marianne Dowell

Portions of this book were written by
Paul Trachtman and Henry Moscow.
Valuable assistance was given by the following departments
and individuals of Time Inc.: Editorial Production,
Norman Airey, Nicholas Costino Jr.; Library, Peter Draz;
Picture Collection, Doris O'Neil; Photographic Laboratory,
George Karas; TIME-LIFE News Service, Murray J. Gart;
Correspondents Friso Endt (Amsterdam), Margot Hapgood
(London), Richard Oulahan (Madrid), Maria Vincenza Aloisi
and Josephine du Brusle (Paris), Anne Callahan (Washington).

The Authors: EDMUND WHITE (Chapters 1, 2 and 3) was a staff writer for TIME-LIFE BOOKS from 1962 to 1970. He is now a senior editor of *Saturday Review* and the author of a novel, *Forgetting Elena.*
DALE BROWN (Chapters 4 and 5) is a writer on the staff of TIME-LIFE BOOKS and is the author of several books including *Wild Alaska* in The American Wilderness series.

The Consultants: Bernard G. Campbell, chief consultant, is Professor of Anthropology at the University of California at Los Angeles. F. Clark Howell is Professor of Anthropology at the University of California at Berkeley.

The Cover: A Homo erectus band crosses an open knoll during mankind's great expansion from the human birthplace in the tropics into the temperate regions of the Old World. Countryside such as this, still bearing traces of early spring snow, lured men on with ample water, plentiful plant foods and the promise of huge grazing herds waiting to be hunted.

The cover scene and the pictures on pages 8 and 23-31 were created by superimposing paintings of Homo erectus on photographs of landscapes like those that are known to have existed when Homo erectus lived.

Contents

Introduction

For many people, exploring the past means no more than looking through old family records in the attic to find glimpses of ancestral homes, and the names and fashions of relatives of times gone by. The more distant past of the human family, a history that goes back not two generations, nor two hundred generations, but twenty thousand generations, is equally fascinating. This series, The Emergence of Man, is an exploration of that intriguing genealogy, and this book picks up the story with the appearance of the first members of the genus *Homo:* the first true men. They appeared on the family tree some 1.3 million years ago, having evolved in the tropics from their pre-human ancestors, the Australopithecines.

The first man, called *Homo erectus,* shares with modern man a great many anatomical and cultural features, including efficient upright walking, the use of fire, specialized tools and, probably, complex social interactions. The success of his life style resulted in the spread of Homo erectus to much of the Old World, and it was during this part of our history that the biological and behavioral mechanisms of modern man evolved. *The First Men* provides an illuminating account of this momentous transformation of our ancestors from nonman to man.

Over the past 80 years facts about the lives of these early men have been exhumed with the utmost care and patience by scientists possessed of great dedication and fortitude—such investigators as the Canadian Davidson Black, who is reported to have died from a lung disease brought on by breathing the rock dust produced while excavating the Peking man fossils, or the Dutchman Eugène Dubois, who left job, home and security to search for, and find, remains of the first men in the jungles of Java.

In only a few areas of science do the visionary and the practical combine as they do in the study of man's past. On the one hand is the romance of the search for and discovery of rare human fossils; on the other, the skill and insight necessary for exhuming those records of the past and for describing and analyzing them in a meaningful fashion. The study of human evolution has drawn to it a number of great scientists, and this book is a testament to their imagination and skill as well as the story of Homo erectus.

The examination of our own past offers a perspective on the present. As we explore the paths our ancestors took in their long evolution, we begin to understand the intricate connections between biological man and cultural man. The archeological and fossil evidence reviewed in this book demonstrates that the existence of Homo erectus was much like that of some hunters and gatherers living today. Thus we see that Homo erectus forged the links between man and his environment into a pattern that has been successful for more than a million years.

Alan Mann
Assistant Professor of Anthropology
University of Pennsylvania

Chapter One: The Great Innovator

On a late spring day 400,000 years ago, a band of about 25 craggy-visaged men, women and children stopped at a sandy cove on the Mediterranean coast. They were looking for a place to stay, and they chose a spot, perched on a sand dune and protected by a limestone cliff, at the mouth of the Paillon Valley. Today, the city of Nice, France, rises around their ancient campsite, but archeologists have unearthed the place, called Terra Amata, where these 25 primitive visitors once made a brief stopover. From the assortment of fossil bones, stone tools and imprints they left and from the consistency of the sand in which they left them, the archeologists have been able to determine that they stayed only about three days and can describe, in extraordinary detail, just what the visitors did there before moving on.

It is possible to tell what kind of shelter they built, what sort of meals they ate, how they made their tools and even, from imprints on the floor of the hut, where they slept and what they slept on. The clues are faint and incomplete, yet they are enough to permit reconstruction of the scene, 400,000 years ago, as these distant ancestors of ours arrived to spend a few days by the sea.

Their first need is a place to stay. As they survey the cove, several men summon the others to a dune where they can see across the valley behind them. From this vantage place they can see a herd of red deer grazing far off in the distance. The men, expert hunters, agree that this is a good spot for a hut. Only a few feet away a clear stream winds by the dune, providing drinking water. The women, picking their way about the edges of the cove, find that the thickets are filled with roots and wild, succulent greens. There is plenty of food at hand.

The group splits up to scour the beach and its bordering brush for the wood and stone they need to build a hut. Driftwood logs, saplings and storm-broken limbs of trees are dragged back to the dune for poles and stakes. There, a few men prune and trim the wood, working with stone hand axes they have carried with them. Soon all the men are working together, driving slender saplings into the sand in the shape of a large oval, almost 50 feet long and 20 feet wide. Within the oval, they sink several larger tree trunks for support posts, and then lash the tops of the saplings together to serve as a tentlike roof. Then, outside the oval, the men pile supporting stones against the wall of the hut, stacking up smaller ones around the big stones.

Now, as everyone gathers inside the hut, the bustle of activity dies away and a hush falls over the group. They watch as an old woman arranges a semicircle of large, rounded pebbles at the center of the hut and fills the shallow pit with dry brush. She is their fire bearer, and it is a critical moment in the life of the group. The old woman lifts the sod cover off a bowl of embers, blows them into life and lights the kindling in the new hearth. They have fire again —flame to cook their meat in, and light that no nighttime predator dare approach.

As the day begins to wane, the women head for the nearby woods to gather the greens for an evening meal. One of the younger women does not follow the

Family-like, a Homo erectus group gathers at a campfire. They are the first humans, distinguished from their forebears by momentous innovations: They are the first to speak, make clothes, build huts, inhabit cold areas, hunt big game and use fire. But perhaps their greatest innovation is a growing sense of kinship leading to the family, foundation of human society.

The seven fossils reproduced in the paintings below include virtually every kind of Homo erectus bone yet found —although some 100 fossils have turned up, all are near duplicates of those shown here. Yet this meager evidence permits reconstruction of an entire skeleton, shown on pages 12-13.

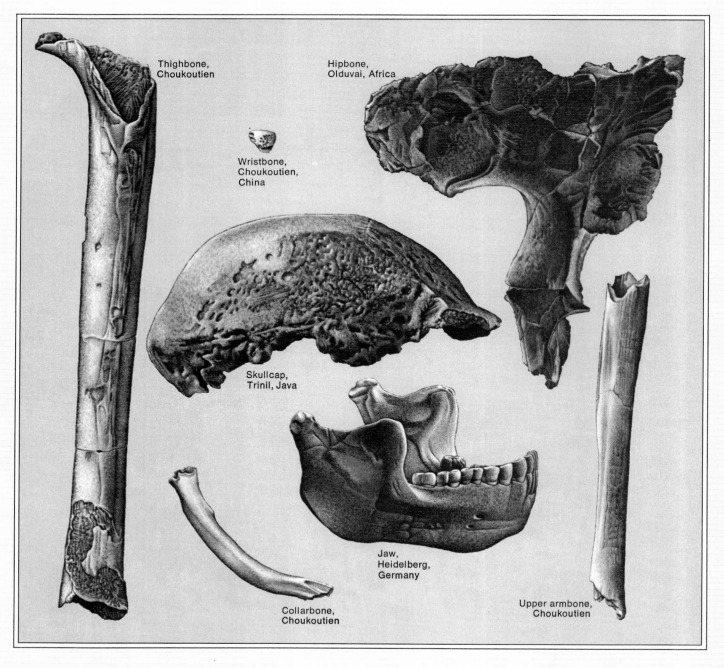

Thighbone,
Choukoutien

Hipbone,
Olduvai, Africa

Wristbone,
Choukoutien,
China

Skullcap,
Trinil, Java

Jaw,
Heidelberg,
Germany

Collarbone,
Choukoutien

Upper armbone,
Choukoutien

gatherers. Instead she leads a group of girls toward the sea, running across the pebbled beach. There, they all venture out into the shallow water of the cove in search of a school of small fish. When they spot one, they wade around it in a semicircle, disturbing the water as little as possible, and, drawing together hip to hip, they drive it toward the shore. As the fish dart through this human net, the women attempt to grab them with their hands until one girl finally catches a fish and flings it onto the beach.

Standing by the hut, a group of hunters suddenly turns toward the woods. Then, grabbing up spears and stones as they go, they take off after a wild boar they have heard crashing through the brush. Inside the hut, in one corner, a toolmaker is already busy turning out new implements from a growing pile of stones he has collected from the beach. As he deftly splits pieces of flint and limestone with sharp blows of a hard quartzite hammerstone, knowing just the angle at which to strike, he quickly lays aside a new supply of simple but sharp-edged cutting and chopping tools. Some he works with special care, tapping away at the edges with the tip of a fire-hardened stag antler to create more delicately flaked and pointed tools. A few young boys surround him, awkwardly trying to imitate his practiced way with the hammerstone, but most of their rocks shatter into useless fragments instead of tools.

Not far from the hut, some older youths who are not yet allowed to hunt with the men practice spear-throwing with sharpened sticks, shouting when a missile lands close to its mark in the sand. They break off their game and rush toward the woods as they see the hunters coming back.

The men and admiring boys return to the dune bearing butchered parts of a wild boar, which are trimmed and prepared for cooking inside the hut with the newly made stone implements. Slabs of meat begin to sizzle on the open hearth as the entire band gathers for a feast. There is charred meat and fish, fruits and greens and a pile of oysters picked up along the shore of the cove.

Soon darkness falls outside. The night air is sweet with the scent of flowering broom and wild thyme, as a misty breeze blows up from the northwest. Animal hides are unrolled and spread out on the sandy floor of the hut, close by the hearth and its warming fire. The walls are drafty, so those who are farthest from the fire wrap themselves in their hides. The fire flickers on all night as they sleep.

What sort of man visited this cove on the coast of Europe 400,000 years ago? Who was he? Although he came each spring for many years, the fossils he left behind him included no human bones—only a single human footprint in the hard sand. Fortunately, there are other sites of similar age where fossil bones of this prehistoric creature have been found, along with similar tools and animal bones and in two instances, hearths. Indeed, when the evidence from all these archeological finds is pieced together, the picture that emerges is remarkably complete, revealing not only what this man looked like, but where he came from. In some ways, with all the advantages of hindsight, scientists probably know more about him than he knew about himself.

He was the first man. He is known, in the scheme of evolution, as *Homo erectus,* or upright man. He was the direct descendant of Australopithecus, a creature considered the missing link between the apes and man. Physically, Homo erectus was quite distinct from his more apelike ancestors. While Australopithecus had evolved a larger brain, relative to his size, than modern apes have and was able to make primitive tools, he was still comparatively small —Pygmy-sized in many cases—and not yet as well adapted as true men are to totally erect posture and walking long distances.

Homo erectus stood straight-backed and walked with a springy stride. He was around five and a half feet tall and owed his manly posture and gait to several developments in the anatomy of his pelvis and foot—changes that had already been apparent in Australopithecus, but that in Homo erectus came close to their modern form. Homo erectus' pelvis was more bowl-shaped, so that the socket at which the femur connects to the pelvis was farther inward than in Australopithecus. This shift gave Erectus a straight-legged stance as opposed to the slightly bowed stance of Australopithecus. In addition, Erectus' foot, arched to support his whole weight, had lost all trace of the ability to grasp that ape feet possess. As a result of these changes, Homo erectus was the first primate who could walk upright for long periods of time without strain.

No complete set of Erectus' hand bones has been found, but his skill at making tools suggests that he had hands like ours, capable of a unique type of grip that sets man apart from other living primates. All primates can use a simple hand grip, with the fingers held together as a hook over some object like a branch. This "power grip" serves well enough for such activities as swinging from a tree limb or grabbing a bunch of greens. Homo erectus' hand was obviously adapted to use the more complicated "pre-

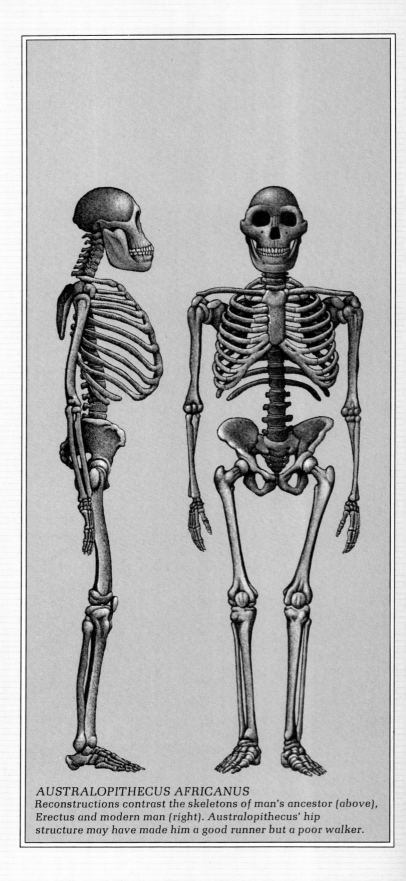

AUSTRALOPITHECUS AFRICANUS
Reconstructions contrast the skeletons of man's ancestor (above), Erectus and modern man (right). Australopithecus' hip structure may have made him a good runner but a poor walker.

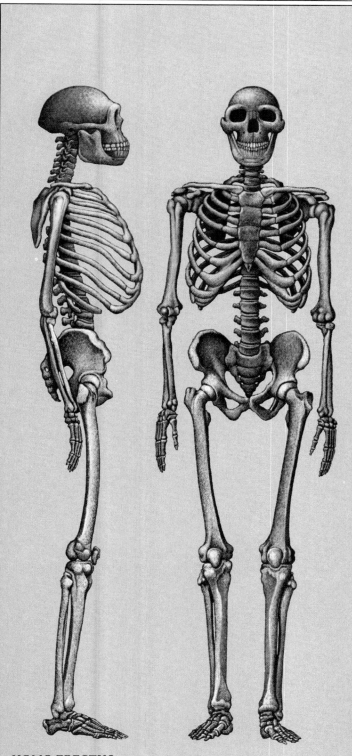

HOMO ERECTUS
A curved spine, short pelvis and head more nearly centered gave the first man erect balance for efficient walking. He was robustly built, five to five and a half feet tall, with thick, heavy bones.

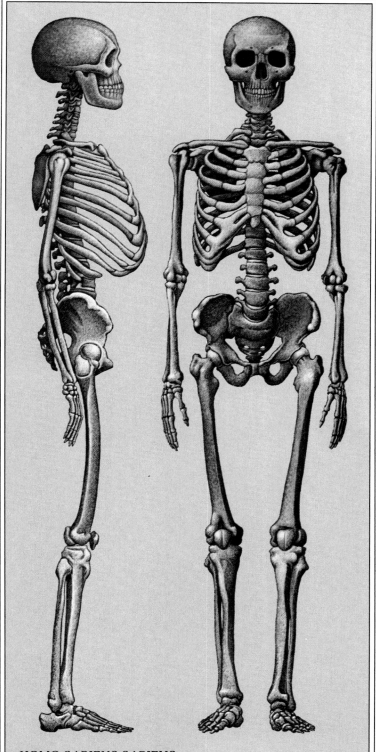

HOMO SAPIENS SAPIENS
A modern man, generally taller than Erectus, has a well-balanced, larger head and longer legs in proportion to his arms. But otherwise his skeleton hardly differs from that of his ancestor.

cision grip," with the thumb and other fingers pressing from opposite sides so that they can hold a needle or throw a spear. Australopithecus had undoubtedly begun to use a version of this grip but because his fingers were thick and his thumb relatively short he would not have been able to use it as effectively as Homo erectus, who must have had thinner and straighter fingers and a longer and more flexible thumb, similar to a modern man's; with the use of what is termed an opposable thumb, his manual dexterity must have been considerable.

While Homo erectus was not built quite like his forebears, neither did he resemble us exactly. His bones were heavier and thicker than a modern man's, and bigger bones required thicker muscles to move them. These skeletal differences, however, were not particularly noticeable. "Below the neck," one expert has noted, "the differences between Homo erectus and today's man could only be detected by an experienced anatomist." From the neck up, however, Erectus looked much more primitive. He had a low, sloping forehead, thick, jutting brows and a massive jaw with only a hint of a chin. Yet, with the exception of his eyebrows, these primitive aspects were less pronounced than they had been in his forebears, and the basic proportions of his head had begun to change. As his brain expanded, his head became higher domed than that of Australopithecus and his forehead receded less. In addition, his jaw became smaller as his demands on it lessened: his diet began to include more easily chewed, cooked food. Taken together these changes tended to humanize his looks; nevertheless his face was probably the least modern thing about him.

In the long progression of primates that led from apelike creatures to man, the changes marking Homo erectus as the first men are matters of degree. Many early anthropologists regarded Australopithecus as very bestial, but the modern view is that man's forebears were far more human than the first apish reconstructions suggested. It follows that the distinctions between Australopithecus and Homo erectus were more subtle than they were once thought to be. Somewhere between early Australopithecus and the first men there were numerous intermediate forms, becoming more and more like humans with succeeding generations. In fact, some classifiers have proposed a separate species, *Homo habilis,* for a creature whom others regard as the last of the Australopithecines. Habilis' brain was slightly larger than that of other Australopithecines, he was a shade taller (about four and a half to five feet tall), and his stance may have been a little more erect. Whether he should be lumped with the Australopithecines or distinguished from them as a separate species of primitive man is an argument best left to the taxonomists. But if we could have seen him with our own eyes, Homo habilis would have looked to us like a creature with a rather apelike head on top of a remarkably human-looking body. His successors, Homo erectus, were different. As one anthropologist has remarked, "they were the first people of whom, if you met them walking across a field, you would say, 'these are definitely not apes, they're men.' "

Far more than increased height, erect stature, manly gait or improved grip, the remarkable change in Homo erectus' brain and behavior clearly marked him as the first of men. The sharpest difference between Homo erectus and all the primates who preceded him was the large size of his brain, and the complexity of behavior this made possible. While the size of the brain case cannot always be relied on as an accurate measure of brain power, it is generally true that among animals of similar size, species with large brains are more intelligent than those with small brains. The capacity of a modern ape's skull—even a great ape like the gorilla—is only about 500 cubic centimeters. The skull capacity of Australopithecus was no larger. Even with the skulls of the disputed Homo habilis included, it seems that the Australopithecine brain case measured between 400 to 660 cubic centimeters. Erectus, however, had a brain case between about 750 and 1,400 cubic centimeters—and the brainier members of the species were well within the range of modern man, whose cranial capacity varies from about 1,000 to 2,000 cubic centimeters.

Homo erectus' brain was not only larger than earlier primate brains, but it was probably far more complex in internal organization. There are no fossil brains to show what the inside of his brain was like, of course, but there is considerable indirect evidence. A comparison of the brains of modern apes and man, for example, shows that the larger human brain has quite different proportions, with larger and more complex individual cells, enlarged centers for such functions as speech, hearing and sight, and many more internal interconnections between brain cells. Scientists consider the internal pattern of organization as important as size in making the human brain what it is. In fact, certain people born with very small brains, a condition known as microcephaly, show distinctly human behavior even though their brains may have a smaller number of cells than does the brain of a healthy gorilla.

This restructuring of the brain was already evident in Australopithecus, for he made tools and showed other signs of manlike behavior, but the great change came with Homo erectus and gave him the mental equipment to distinguish him as a man. The proof lies in what he did with his better brain. In some ways, he simply went further along paths his forebears had begun to tread. In other ways, his accomplishments were unique. He was much more successful than Australopithecus at making tools and at planning and coordinating his hunts.

From the bones of the animals that the first men brought back to their primeval campsites, it is clear they were patient and premeditating hunters, able to lie in wait where they knew their prey would pass or to spread out stealthily and encircle some swift and leaping beast. By such means, the first men brought down gazelles and antelopes, tangled with saber-toothed cats, and at last could hunt down even the goliaths of the grasslands, the elephants.

Homo erectus' increasing concentration on hunting also led to the development of a social organization that is clearly human, being based on a distinct division of labor between men who hunted and women who picked and gathered food. The women were probably less promiscuous than their female forebears, and the men more possessive about mates. Although it is unlikely that anyone had connected sexual coupling with the mysteries of childbirth, the first men probably had a casual but well-defined family life. Some anthropologists believe that siblings and aunts may even have served as baby-sitters, so that young mothers would have been able to leave their infants from time to time to help with the work of gathering food.

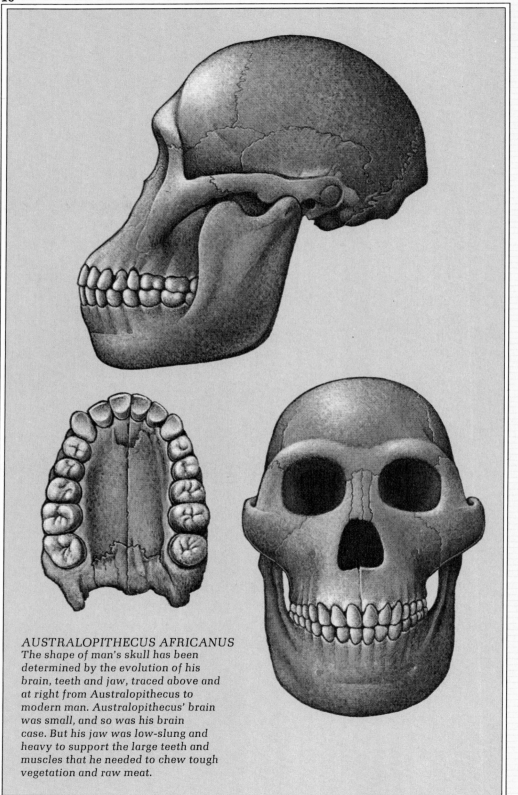

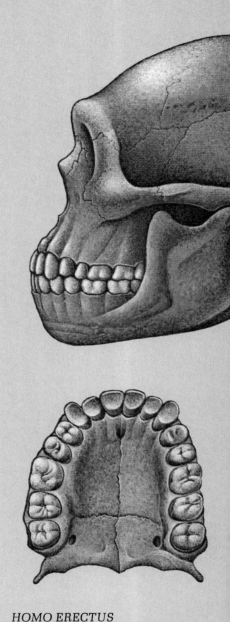

AUSTRALOPITHECUS AFRICANUS
The shape of man's skull has been determined by the evolution of his brain, teeth and jaw, traced above and at right from Australopithecus to modern man. Australopithecus' brain was small, and so was his brain case. But his jaw was low-slung and heavy to support the large teeth and muscles that he needed to chew tough vegetation and raw meat.

HOMO ERECTUS
Homo erectus had a much larger brain than Australopithecus; his brain case had to be twice as big to hold it. His teeth—particularly the molars in back —were smaller in relation to his jaw, an adaptation to his diet of softer, cooked food. The teeth also lay in a shorter, wider arch, in a jaw that was larger than Australopithecus', but smaller relative to skull size.

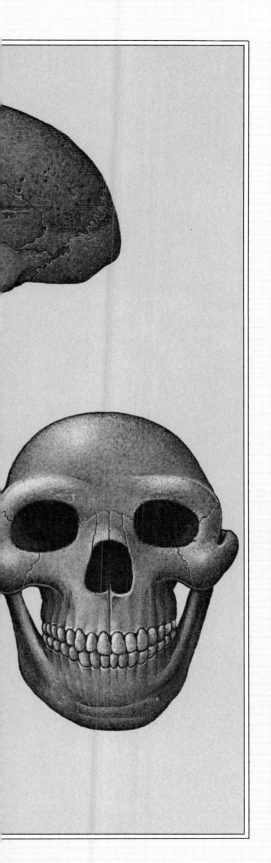

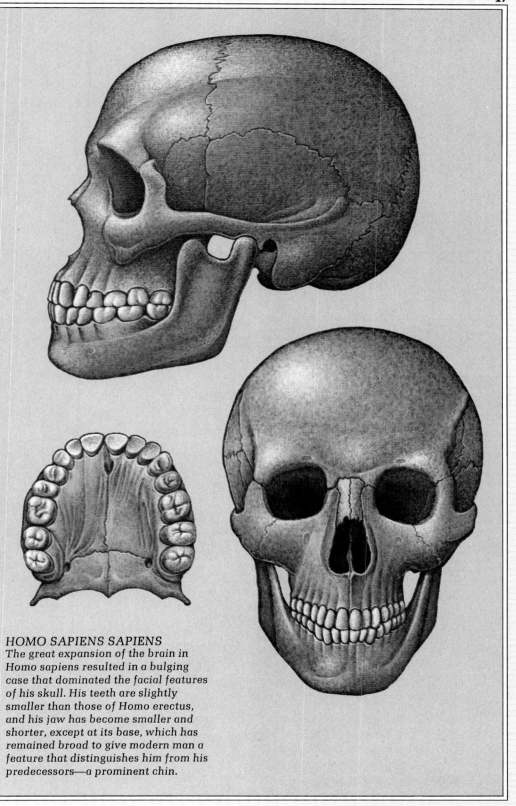

HOMO SAPIENS SAPIENS
The great expansion of the brain in Homo sapiens resulted in a bulging case that dominated the facial features of his skull. His teeth are slightly smaller than those of Homo erectus, and his jaw has become smaller and shorter, except at its base, which has remained broad to give modern man a feature that distinguishes him from his predecessors—a prominent chin.

But the creation of human society is only one of the great accomplishments that give Homo erectus his place as the first among men. He spread out over much of the world, making his way into the wintry climates of the north where there is no evidence that a monkey or ape had ever survived before. He mastered fire, using it to cook, to warm himself and even to trap big game. And he learned to talk. Australopithecus must have been capable of making expressive sounds that others around him could comprehend. But although his system of communication was considerably more advanced than that of the apes, he still did not use words. From the development of Homo erectus' brain, and from changes that probably occurred in his vocal tract, it seems that he was capable of some rudimentary human speech.

Modern man can produce a great variety of distinct sounds when he speaks. This ability depends on several unique features of the modern vocal tract: the pharynx can vary its volume by more than 10 times to produce different sounds in quick succession; the tongue is set far back in the throat; and the jaws are relatively small—which leaves more room in the pharynx for talking, and less for chewing, swallowing and breathing. The anatomy of Homo erectus' vocal tract was probably more like an ape's, smaller and less flexible than a modern human one. He could make some of the sounds we use in speaking but not all, and it appears that he could communicate at only about one tenth the rate of modern man. (But then, he didn't choke as easily.) The fact that he could talk at all was probably his greatest gift. It means that man could communicate symbolically and refer to objects and ideas in speech. The development of language, described in Chapter Four, distinguished

man as a uniquely cultural animal—one who could compete much more effectively in the struggle for existence by adapting his behavior, more than his body, to new and changing conditions.

The achievements of these first men, as they spread their kind and their culture across the far reaches of the Old World, is written in a varied fossil record—a story told in fragments found thousands of miles apart. When the fragments are put together, the story they tell is remarkable. It is as if scientists had found a multitude of verse fragments from Homer's ancient epic, the *Odyssey,* and put them all together to see who Odysseus was, how he lived and where he went on his voyages by sea.

Sometime about 1.3 million years ago, perhaps in several places at several times, the advanced Australopithecines gave birth to the earliest bands of Homo erectus. The oldest remains have been found in the tropics—in Africa and Java. As the populations of Homo erectus multiplied, some of the first men stayed on in the tropics, developing the skills, language and social organization that enabled them to flourish as hunters of big game on the savannas. But as their numbers increased, men spread out. They probably did not migrate in the sense of pulling up stakes and moving hundreds of miles to a new location. Rather some members of the band would settle some miles away from the rest, and years later yet another group would move farther off still. Over centuries and millennia, this slow process took Erectus northward out of the lush tropics. The problems and challenges of surviving in a severe and wintry world stimulated new cultural and social adaptations, and, in all probability, even speeded up the evolution of the species.

Homo erectus' dispersion across several continents occurred during a time of great change in the world's geography and climates: the Ice Age. In a series of epic cold waves, snow-fed glaciers spread over the northern continents, while rainfall may have increased greatly in the tropics. But between these cold spells, the glaciers melted away and temperatures were often warmer in Europe and Asia than they are today, while the tropics may have experienced long periods of drought.

At times, with so much of the world's water locked up in ice and snow, sea levels dropped greatly and land bridges between continents appeared. Java, now an island in the Indonesian archipelago, was for a time connected to the Asian mainland. Similarly, Africa might have been linked to Europe across Sicily for a time, while tropical rains are believed to have produced great stretches of grassland and lakes in the once impassable North African desert. Experts disagree about exactly when and where these land bridges appeared, and which ones Homo erectus used —but somehow he was successful, moving across thousands of miles to inhabit most of the Old World. When the first men reached the northern parts of the world—and what routes they took to get there—is still a matter of considerable debate among the experts. In part, the problem is the age of skulls and skeletons found in various regions of the world, for evidence on this point has kept changing as new and improved methods of dating fossils are applied to the various finds. It is possible, however, to sketch out a reasonable picture of events based on the best evidence now available.

At the time when Homo erectus evolved from the Australopithecines there was a vast tropical corridor of woodland and savanna surrounding the Indian Ocean, running up the east coast of Africa across the Indian subcontinent and down into the Indonesian archipelago. Australopithecus lived in many parts of this corridor, either dispersing through it or repeatedly evolving from his ancestors in several of its parts. He was firmly established in both Africa and Asia before Homo erectus evolved, so it is impossible to say whether Homo erectus first appeared in the east or west.

Like his forebears, Homo erectus probably drifted back and forth throughout the tropics, with new bands budding off from settled populations as man's numbers increased. Some of these new bands also shifted north, probably along several different routes at different times. Some dispersed north from Java on the long passage to China; others spread north from Africa across land bridges to Europe, or entered Europe after skirting the Mediterranean by way of the Middle East, across Turkey and up the Danube into Hungary. As the map on page 111 suggests, Homo erectus may also have reached Europe by drifting across the Indian subcontinent from Java and may have reached China along a path from Europe across Russia and Tibet.

Whenever it began, the expansion from the tropics into Europe had been completed by a million years ago and into China perhaps even as early as 750,000 years ago. Living sites that old have been unearthed in several places where man first felt the chill of northern winters. The oldest hearths, going back some 750,000 years, may be those in a cave at Escale, in southern France, and the evidence suggests that fire was also used in China at least 500,000 years ago. What led the first men to brave the winters in these places can only be guessed. It may have been the pressures of multiplying human populations; it may have been man's search for new hunting grounds. In any case changes in the world's geography facilitated the expansion to the north.

Once man became so widely dispersed, however, he was forced to adapt to a new and broader diversity of changing climates and environments. Homo erectus was probably forced to retreat from his northern outposts many times during the coldest millennia of this changeable age. The fossil record clearly shows that hundreds of animal species, less adaptable and peripatetic than man, perished during the times of advancing ice. And, as one expert has noted, "as zones of climate moved back and forth, the animals adjusted to particular geographic zones must have been herded and driven and shoved around the face of the earth to an exceptional degree."

Confronted with such trying conditions, the first men were forced to meet the challenge of winter with their wits. They discovered how to use fire to their advantage. They learned to carry it from the wilds, where it appeared when a volcano erupted, when lightning struck in the dry grass of the plains or when some outcrop of coal or shale oil burst into flames by spontaneous combustion. Having captured fire, the first men learned to keep it going in their hearths. Their fires must have died out many times before they invented methods for preserving their embers, perhaps banking them with sod (as is still done in some remote corners of the world where the matchstick has not made its appearance). Once the first men had mastered fire, they began to live by it—for they could not have survived in the north without it.

Excavations at the great cave of Choukoutien, near Peking, have given a remarkable view of the importance of fire to the first men. When Homo erectus first arrived there about half a million years ago, the caves in the Peking hills were inhabited by bears and a variety of other beasts. The men must have spent their first few winters at Choukoutien along the crevices and ledges of the cliff, wrapping themselves in hides while building some sort of makeshift shelters against the bitter winds. Except for the cold, it was the kind of spot the first men picked out wherever they settled: it was not far from water (a river flowed by the foot of the cliff) and it gave them a commanding view of a grassy plain where herds of animals could be spotted as they grazed.

The great cave in the cliff offered a good place to come in from the cold, but the men had to fight the animals around them for possession of it. The oldest and deepest layers of fossils in the cave show that Homo erectus made his home there, and was driven out again, over many generations. Human and animal occupation of the cave alternated fairly regularly, as man's place was preempted by such large carnivores as cave bears, saber-toothed cats and giant hyenas. At a certain point, however, the fossil deposits show that man took full and permanent possession of the cave —and this is the point at which the evidence of fire becomes continuous. Gradually, fire had become the key to man's control of the cave. His flaming brands and the light of his all-night fires kept even the most savage predators at bay.

Besides the protection it afforded, fire was a key to survival in other ways. Once Homo erectus discovered the art of cooking—perhaps by accident as a slab of meat fell onto a flaming hearth and was eaten—he seems to have cooked much of what he caught. The Choukoutien cave floor was littered with charred bones of sheep, large horses, pig, buffalo and deer. Cooked meat was not only more appetizing and tender: it increased the value of the food to man, for heat breaks down complex compounds of tough meat and releases nutritious juices.

Besides cooking with fire, Homo erectus discovered other practical uses for it. It broadened his choice of tools and weapons. The observation that bone or antler grew hard in the heat of a campfire, or that green wood did not always burn completely and instead hardened must have led him to employ fire in toolmaking. Among the bones fossilized at Choukoutien were pieces of fire-hardened tips of antlers, which probably served as hammers for chipping away the rough edges of split-stone tools and fashioning cutting edges onto them; the points of wooden spears found at other sites were also hardened in fire to increase their piercing power. Similarly sticks could be tempered with flame before they were sharpened for use as digging implements.

Despite such improvements in technology, Homo erectus seems to have been slow to learn the secret of making his own fire, if he ever learned at all. Perhaps one day as someone sat striking rock against rock, sparks flew onto dry moss or grass and caused flames to spring up. However, only certain rocks, such as flint and iron pyrites used in combination, produce the necessary sparks and no such firestones have so far been found among the relics Homo erectus left behind. The earliest known firestone, a round lump of iron pyrites, grooved by repeated strikings, dates back only 15,000 years, hundreds of thousands of years after the last of the first men. Even in modern times some primitive hunter-gatherers have not known how to make fire.

Nevertheless, once man learned to use and control fire, the idea is believed to have caught on rapidly, at least throughout the northern world. On the winterless plains of Africa, where men could thrive in the open without any need of fire, relics of its use date back to only about 50,000 years ago.

The men who occupied the cave at Choukoutien left an impressive record of how they conducted their lives in the north. By and large their basic tools and weapons were not much different from those their relatives were using several thousand miles away in Africa and Europe—the same stone scrapers, choppers and hammers. Erectus was apparently making many implements of bone as well—a detailed inspection of his bone industry suggests that he was using long bones for clubs and spears, making daggers out of elephant tusks and antelope horns, and otherwise splintering skeletons into primitive shovels, picks, chisels, knives and the like; it has even been suggested that Erectus used skull caps for bowls.

There is yet another story written in the bones. Much that is known about these first men provides a portrait of our Paleolithic ancestors as solid and industrious social human beings, sharing the burdens of a primitive existence. Yet, among the fossils unearthed on the floor of their cave, there are reminders that the men of Peking were savages, living in a savage world and ungoverned by conventions of civilized society. Human skulls were found bashed in at the base, and many other human bones were charred. From this evidence, some archeologists conclude that the first men practiced cannibalism. Savage as this act is now considered, it does not necessarily make Erectus less human. In fact, it could be taken as evidence of a forward step in man's development.

In all the primitive tribes that have been known to practice cannibalism, it is always carried out not for the sake of food, but as a mystic ritual act. As the German anthropologist G. H. R. von Koenigswald has explained, "The head hunter is not content merely to possess the skull, but opens it and takes out the brain, which he eats in order by this means to acquire the wisdom and skill of his foe." From the evidence suggesting that the first men ate each other, it might even be concluded that they had some spiritual notions that cannibalism could increase their powers.

How is it possible to tell so much about these long-vanished ancestors of ours? Even a few decades ago no one could possibly have said with any assurance that Homo erectus was the first man, or described in any detail his wanderings and ways as he spread from the tropics to the temperate zones of the Old World. A hundred years ago no one had yet found a single fossil of Homo erectus, and there was no scientific proof that he had ever existed.

The story of Homo erectus—who he was, where and when he lived, and what he did in his time on earth—can now be told because a small band of determined scientists spent their lives discovering these facts. Parts of the tale came to light in widely scattered corners of the world—fossils, artifacts and living sites were found at different times by men who sometimes did not recognize the real meaning of their discoveries. Some of the discoveries, indeed, provoked bitter and prolonged controversies among the experts. But in recent years the quantity of evidence accumulated by the fossil hunters has come to be recognized as the portrait of a distinct species—a record left behind by the first men and assembled by his modern ancestors in an extraordinary tale of scientific detection.

Fire, the Magic Tool

Nothing so marks Homo erectus as a man, the first true human, as his use of fire. Once he dared turn this destructive natural force to his own good, he found his life changed, his horizons broadened. He could cook his food, increasing its digestibility and value as sustenance. He could keep himself warm in the cold, ward off predators and light up the dark.

Significantly, the earliest conclusive evidence of man's use of fire comes not from his birthplace in the tropics —where year round the days are almost equal in length and the sun provides heat enough—but from the French cave of L'Escale. Hearths there may date back 750,000 years.

Driven by curiosity, but restrained by fear, a hunter braves the fierce heat to approach an awe-inspiring source of fire—molten lava.

Stealing Flame from Nature

Living during a period of great instability in the earth's crust, Homo erectus would have been eyewitness to eruptions and lava flows. He would also have seen conflagrations started by lightning, as in the picture at right, or by spontaneous combustion of coal- or oil-shale deposits. His initial reaction to such spectacular phenomena was, without doubt, terror—but eventually he dared come close to the flames. Perhaps an act as simple as picking up a burning stick to frighten away a predator led to the discovery that fire was useful—and could be tamed. But how to preserve it?

Blaze after blaze must have gone out before Homo erectus learned to take fire with him in his wanderings so he could light new fires, perhaps carrying live coals somehow, or fashioning slow-burning torches. There is no doubt he learned to keep his home fires burning: in China's Choukoutien caves, where Homo erectus dwelt 400,000 years ago, archeologists found one hearth with ashes piled 22 feet deep, an indication that the fire there had been nurtured for generations.

Coming upon a blaze started accidentally by lightning in a pine forest, a group of hunters show mixed

reactions. Some, more *fascinated* than *intimidated* by *the blaze, find that they can capture fires of their own by sticking branches into the flames.*

After setting a fast-moving fire in a pine forest, hunters pick off deer fleeing the flames. The drastic herding technique not only required skill and

A Weapon to Overpower Foe or Prey

Even the most ferocious of animals are afraid of fire, a fact Homo erectus undoubtedly realized from the start. Once he overcame his own fear of the flames and began using them to frighten predators from his campsites and to drive bears and saber-toothed cats out of caves, he must have wakened to the possibility of hunting with fire as well. By igniting the dry floor of a forest or the brittle grass of a plain, he could flush animals hidden there into the open, where he had a chance to kill even the largest. One method he apparently used required the setting of a semicircle of fire behind his prey. As the flames moved along, some of the animals, more terrified of the fire than of the men, would dash through the blaze: the hunters could then fall on them with spears, clubs, and stone axes.

The hunters' alliance with fire was a tricky one. The men, always in danger of being caught in their own trap, must have used their weapon warily. Learning to plan the fire hunt carefully would have demanded much of Homo erectus' slowly developing intelligence—but the fire hunt's great value must also have helped spur him on to further achievements.

cooperation, but also involved some risk—sparks could start smaller blazes and trap the hunters.

Cooking, a Revolution in Eating

Homo erectus must have known from experience that the meat of an animal that had been killed in a fire took on attractive qualities, not only tasting good, but also requiring less effort to chew. It would not have been hard for him to make the connection between cause and effect and to start deliberately tossing pieces of raw, butchered prey into the flames of his campfires.

Once cooking became established practice, it revolutionized Homo erectus' life. One immediate gain was an increase in the available food supply. The protein and fats of meat provide more energy in a more compact form than vegetable food; but most primates are essentially vegetarian and their digestive systems cannot handle raw meat well. Fire partially breaks down the meat before it gets to the stomach and makes it easier to digest. Thus cooking made available to man a much more efficient diet as well as increasing the number of items on his menu. Cooked meat is also easier to chew so that weaker members of the band—the aged or sick—could handle it, prolonging their lives.

The strangest result of the invention of cooking was a change in appearance. Since man no longer had to chew his food so hard, his teeth gradually became smaller, his jaw grew shorter, the massive bony structure needed to support the heavy jaw muscles dwindled in size—and his face started to approach its modern look.

After butchering their prey where they killed it and carrying the meat back to camp in manageable

chunks, hunters hack it into still smaller pieces before throwing it into the fire. They apparently shared the meat, made more digestible by cooking.

The Hearth, Cradle of Language

With tamed fire came a new sociability for early man. Drawn to the flames for warmth and protection from animals, groups of men, women and children found their day extended after darkness fell. In the security of the campfire, they could work on their weapons and tools, cook, eat and sleep—probably, in cold regions, clustered as close to the hot ashes as they dared. Thus the hearth, whether outdoors or in a cave, became the focus for companionship and an increasingly family-oriented life. Furthermore, having to tend the hearth continually lest the fire die out reinforced the growing importance of a home base, a place, however impermanent, where the women could take care of the children and to which the hunters could return. As this sense of domesticity grew, the members of the band must have been stimulated by mutual needs and experiences to verbalize more and more—thus hastening, in the comforting glow of the campfire, the all-important evolution of language.

At day's end, a part of a band shares the warming glow of a campfire. Within its safe circle of light and

stimulated by a communal spirit, the members of the Erectus group, with slow speech and expressive gestures, review the luck of the day's hunt.

Chapter Two: The Mystery of the First Men

Dutch anthropologist Eugène Dubois, serving as an army doctor in Java, discovered the first fossils of the earliest true men in 1891.

In the early 1870s a distinguished German scientist toured Holland, lecturing on the new theory of man's descent from the prehistoric apes. The talks stirred great interest, but they also provoked doubt and opposition. At Roermond, a young high school student named Eugène Dubois went to hear the lecture. It was a fascinating theory, the boy thought, even if there were no facts to prove it.

At the time there was hardly a scrap of evidence to show that the gentlemen and ladies of the Victorian age had evolved from some apish primate of the past. Moreover, in the years when Eugène Dubois was still a schoolboy, much was going on in the world that made it hard for people to accept the apes as ancestors. It was an age of human progress and accomplishment. In England people could still parade through the glitter of the Crystal Palace, which had opened in 1851 as a dazzling monument to man's achievements. America was entering its own Gilded Age, taking pride in its self-made millionaires. In many cities, people had running water and lighted streets, and a number of new inventions were making life easier and more civilized. There were iceboxes, sewing machines, elevated railways, lawn mowers, typewriters and even telephones; in fact, young Dubois spent one of his school vacations installing a telephone in his parents' house—a novelty at the time in Holland.

In this atmosphere of progress and self-approval, the claim that man was merely an offshoot of the apes was rejected by much of the public and by many eminent scientists as well. People were beginning to accept the idea of evolution—but only as it applied to the lower animals. Scientists agreed that the world was very old and that geologic strata provided a clear record of past ages on earth. They accepted Darwin's thesis that modern species of animals were descendants of more primitive ancestors, for the lines of descent could be traced in the fossils clearly visible in ancient beds of rock. In fact, there were some fossil remains of apes showing their evolution from prehistoric to modern forms. But the evolution of man was something else. No one had yet found any fossils proving a link between the apes and man. Most of those who doubted man's primate origins did so not merely because of a blind acceptance of the Biblical account of Creation, but simply because there was no convincing evidence to support Darwin.

In the existing fossil record, a German scientist of the time observed, man "appears at once as a complete *Homo sapiens.*" The distinguished director of Berlin's Geological and Paleontological Institute assured everyone that paleontology—the science of fossils—"knows no ancestors of man."

Some scientists took the lack of any fossils of intermediate manlike apes as proof that no such creatures had ever existed. At the other extreme, some of Darwin's early supporters rushed forward with fanciful pedigrees for man, making up in enthusiasm for what they lacked in evidence. Even believers in human evolution were confused by the outpouring of rival experts' family trees for man, full of imaginary apish ancestors with scientific-sounding Greek and Latin names.

In this atmosphere of often vituperous debate over man's origins, Eugène Dubois completed his schooling and began an academic career as instructor in anatomy at the Royal Normal School in Amsterdam. His professional specialty qualified him to take a more than casual interest in what was then the most prominent of scientific controversies, and he was fascinated by the many different family trees that were being published in learned—and popular—journals. But he also realized that armchair speculation would never really prove anything about man's distant past. To establish man's place in evolution, someone would have to find a fossil of a primitive creature that was the clear forerunner of man on earth.

At the age of 29 Eugène Dubois set out to find such a fossil. By then a lecturer at the University of Amsterdam, he dismayed his colleagues by taking off for the wilds of Sumatra, where, he said, he had reason to believe he would solve the mystery of man's origins. While his elders on the faculty sadly protested this touch of madness in an otherwise sober and promising young man, Dubois' departure in 1887 marked the start of the greatest manhunt in the history of science—the search for our ancestors.

In the century since Dubois began this search, it has turned up a host of fossil skulls and skeletons of our primitive forebears—but it is only in recent years that scientists have been able to sort out the evidence and fit the pieces into a clear and comprehensible story. It is now known that the first true men belonged to one species, called *Homo erectus,* and that they evolved over a million years ago from a more apelike genus called *Australopithecus.* There are now well-established methods, such as comparisons of teeth or cranial capacity, for deciding whether a fossil skull belonged to a man or an apelike predecessor, and many new and accurate methods of dating a fossil's age. But in the early years of the search, each new fossil find seemed to raise more questions than it resolved, and each skull was seen by its discoverer as representing a separate species of early man. Hu-

man fossils found in Java, Peking and Heidelberg, for example, were each given a separate place in the scheme of human evolution, and each was named for the place where it was found. There are indeed some fine anatomical distinctions between Java man, Peking man, Heidelberg man and others in the collection of human ancestors, but all are now seen as far-flung representatives of the species *Homo erectus.* Their differences are recognized today as minor ones, the sort of variation that can be found among the living races of modern man. It is easy enough to see their close relationship after the fact, when all the fossils can be laid out and compared. But the early enthusiastic fossil hunters had only their spades and their speculations to go on, and the trail of discovery that lay before them was more often than not strewn with false leads and unexpected twists.

When Eugène Dubois made his fateful decision to go fossil hunting, he was not looking for the first man at all. He wanted to find fossil evidence of a "missing link"—a creature with both apelike and human traits that would prove the relationship of man and the apes. Dubois' boyhood had prepared him in many ways for the adventure. Born in 1858 in Eijsden, Holland, he had spent much of his early youth outdoors, exploring fields and woods near his home, and roaming along the banks of the Maas River. Although the Dubois family was quite conventional and religious (one of Eugène's sisters became a nun), the home atmosphere was not one of narrow-minded provincial piety. The boy's pharmacist father stirred his interest in science by teaching him the Latin names of each tree, shrub, grass, moss and lichen in the surrounding area. Young Dubois even did some amateur fossil hunting in a limestone quarry near his home. His pockets, a relative remembered, were always crammed with rocks, rabbit skulls and small skeletons. Dubois went on to medical school and then chose academic life over medical practice. For six years he delivered his lectures and gave no hint of the wild idea that was taking hold of him. As he read each new scientific paper on the origins of man and tried to draw his own conclusions, he kept returning to the thought that somewhere there must be a fossil that would end the speculation and set the record straight once and for all. But where?

Dubois began his detective work by going over all the clues he could find. One important clue was the existence of human fossils unearthed in a limestone cave in a gorge in Germany, locally known as the Neanderthal. The first of these fossils had been discovered in 1856—two years before Dubois was born—and for 12 years the Neanderthal remains were the only trace of a primitive skeleton in the human closet. The Neanderthal skull had some definitely primitive and rather apelike features, including a low crown, receding forehead and heavy eyebrow ridges. These characteristics seemed to make the gap between modern man and the apes less pronounced, and provided some support for the theory of man's animal origins. But while some experts assumed Neanderthals to have been very primitive characters, not even Darwin's strongest supporters classified them as missing links. Because of their large brain cases, most scientists maintained they were simply the remains of modern men who had somehow been oddly deformed, or that they were a strange, extinct race of modern man.

Dubois, a firm believer in evolution, considered the Neanderthal fossils to be definitely human but very ancient. To him they suggested that the search for even more primitive creatures should be carried out in some region of limestone deposits and caves, similar to the habitat of the Neanderthal; but they also suggested that Europe was not the place to look for a missing link. The missing links, he reasoned, must have lived long before the Neanderthals, at a time when Europe was far too cold to permit their survival. The forebear Dubois wanted to find, he concluded, must have lived in a tropical part of the world untouched by the glaciers of the ice age.

There were other clues as well that pointed to the tropics. Darwin had suggested that our tree-dwelling progenitors lived in "some warm, forest-clad land." Alfred Russel Wallace, an English biologist who had independently proposed precisely the same theory of evolution as Darwin, had also suggested that man's forebears would be found in a tropical zone. Wallace had lived in Malaysia for eight years, and he had noticed that the islands of Sumatra and Borneo were the home of both the gibbon, the oldest and most primitive living apes, and the orangutan, one of the most advanced and intelligent species of ape.

Dubois was especially excited by a passage he came across while reading Wallace's book, *Malay Archipelago, The Land of the Orang-utan and the Bird of Paradise: Narrative of Travel with Studies of Man and Nature,* published in 1869. "It is very remarkable," Wallace wrote, "that an animal, so large, so peculiar, and of such a high type of form as the orangutan, should be confined to so limited a district—to two islands. . . . With what interest must every naturalist look forward to the time when the caves of the tropics be thoroughly examined, and the past

A Boyhood of Cave Exploration

Eugène Dubois, born in 1858, began life in the sleepy town of Eijsden (right), bordering the Maas River in the south of Holland. His later archeological exploits in Sumatra and Java were prefigured by his early fascination with rocks and wildlife found along the banks of the Maas.

Among the places the boy explored was a deep limestone cave in a nearby mountain known as the St. Pietersberg. The cave (opposite) had been mined of its stone for centuries to build local houses, but it was still a wonderland of fossils, bats, unusual plants and mysterious graffiti, and it sparked the interest in fossils documented in the photographs on these and the following pages. All but two of the pictures are from a collection preserved by Dubois' family.

Eijsden, when Dubois was a boy, consisted of a cluster of provincial Dutch homes.

The Duboises' house boasted a separate carriage entrance (left).

In this 1886 picture, young Eugène is behind his sister, a nun.

A cave in the St. Pietersberg attracted Dubois as a fossil source.

An 1883 photograph shows Dubois as a teacher in Amsterdam.

In the St. Pietersberg cave, Dubois found these curious figures and symbols, carved into the limestone during the Middle Ages.

history and earliest appearance of the great man-like apes be at length made known." Wallace's curiosity about these islands and their caves proved contagious, and Dubois began to think seriously of going to the Dutch East Indies to explore these caves himself. The more he read about the geology and natural history of the region, the more convinced he became that the missing link would be discovered there.

Dubois' planning focused on Sumatra, which was then under Dutch rule and therefore a practical place for a Dutch citizen to launch an archeological expedition. In 1886 he told some of his colleagues at the University of Amsterdam what he had in mind. They were shocked and tried to dissuade him. He was highly regarded on the faculty and seemed to be throwing away the promise of a distinguished career as a professor. One older colleague called his plan the wild fancy of an overimaginative mind, politely suggesting that Dubois had taken leave of his senses. Moreover, he had married one of his students that year and they were expecting their first child. Dubois' wife, an attractive and popular girl, may have wondered whether the Sumatran jungles were a fit place to raise children. But, as their son later wrote, she shared with her husband "a firm belief in his ambitions." No one else did.

Having made up his mind, Dubois quit his teaching post and spent many discouraging months doggedly seeking financial backing for his expedition. He was turned down flatly by private philanthropists and government bureaucrats alike. Finally, seeing he had no other way to get to Sumatra, Dubois enlisted as a doctor in the Dutch East Indian Army. After a seven-week voyage aboard a Royal Dutch Mail packet, he arrived in Padang, Sumatra, with his wife and the daughter who had been born to them shortly before their departure.

For two years Dubois was assigned to a small hospital in the interior of the island, and his duties attending the few sick soldiers left him more than enough time to explore the surrounding region. At his own expense, he investigated a great many limestone caves and deposits, but all of the fossils he turned up were too recent to interest him.

One of his searches nearly cost him his life. Crawling into a narrow-mouthed cave on the side of a hill, he had to move forward on his belly while holding a candle in his hand. A peculiar, unpleasant odor and the sight of pieces of bones strewn about made him stop abruptly. He had crawled into a tiger's den. Luckily, the tiger was away, but as Dubois tried to back out of the cave he got stuck in the low, narrow entrance and could not dislodge himself. He called frantically for help, but the natives accompanying him had wandered off. Just when Dubois was convinced that his own bones would soon be added to those in the cave, the natives finally returned and pulled him out by his feet.

In 1890, after an attack of malaria, he was transferred to the drier climate of neighboring Java and placed on inactive duty. Now he was free to spend all of his time on research. The colonial government, showing a new interest in his work, even supplied him with a native crew of convict laborers and two Dutch officers to oversee them. With such backing, excavations proceeded on a grand scale.

Dubois and his family established a home and headquarters in a spacious tropical house—the former home of a government official—in the small town of Tulungagung in east Java. From there Dubois di-

To the Indies in Search of Fossils

The S.S. Princess Amalia, with the Duboises aboard, left for Sumatra in October 1887.

Before departing with his wife, Anna, Dubois grew a beard.

Dubois in uniform (upper left) and wife (center) begin the trip.

rected several digging parties at different locations. The region was extraordinarily rich in fossils of many kinds, and Dubois was soon dividing his time between visiting the sites and sorting through the fossils sent back to his home. Boxes of fossils packed in dried teak leaves piled up on the front gallery of the house, from which they were eventually shipped to the Netherlands (by 1894, Dubois had shipped off 400 cases of fossil bones, including specimens of many extinct and previously unknown animals).

At one site to the north, Dubois' foreman reported an unexpected problem. He found that natives had been digging up fossils in the area for many years and selling them to Chinese merchants as dragon's bones to be ground into powder for an ancient and popular Chinese cure-all (in addition to fossilized bone, the ingredients for this medicine included tiger's claws and whiskers, bat dung and rhinoceros horn). The local fossil hunters, unwilling to give up such a profitable business with the Chinese, would not sell any of their finds to Dubois' party. To make matters worse, the foreman soon discovered that his own workmen were stealing the fossils they unearthed and carrying them off at night to sell to the local traders. In one instance a perfectly preserved elephant skull, turned up at the end of a day's digging but not quite freed from its bed of rock, was gone the next morning when the foreman arrived there. Unable to stop the thefts himself, the foreman finally appealed to the colonial government, which issued an order outlawing the sale of any fossils to Chinese merchants in Java.

To Dubois, the most promising site seemed to be an exposed and stratified embankment along the Solo River, near the small village of Trinil. Here, in the months when the river was low, he could survey a 45-foot-high bank of ancient river deposits, clearly defined layers of fine volcanic debris and sandstone. In August 1891 his workers began digging down through the strata with hoes, hammers and chisels. The implements and methods used by these workers were crude by later standards (pages 87-95), but Dubois was one of the first scientists ever to attempt such a systematic search for fossils. As the upper layers were removed, a rich harvest of ancient bones appeared, and in September the first fossil of a primitive primate was found—a single, apelike tooth.

On first inspection, this fossil seemed to Dubois the wisdom tooth of an extinct giant chimpanzee. Later, in comparing it with molars of other apes, he noted a strange wrinkling of the crown, suggesting the tooth of an orangutan. As Dubois mulled over the molar, the digging went on for another month. Then, only three feet from where the tooth had turned up, and in exactly the same layer, a workman uncovered a heavy, chocolate brown "rock" that looked like a turtle's shell. Dubois was called over to the spot at once and carefully picked it up. Turning it in his hand, he could not quite tell what it was, but as he slowly scratched away some of the stony matter encrusting it, the shell looked more and more like part of a skull. After detailed study of both the skullcap and the tooth Dubois reported in a government mining bulletin that carried periodic accounts of his work: "That both specimens come from a great manlike ape was at once clear."

Shortly after these finds, the rains came, the river rose and digging had to be suspended until the following year. Dubois studied the skull all winter, but despite his expert knowledge of anatomy he found it

Text continued on page 44

A Welcome in Java

An old photograph shows a riverside street in Surabaya, Java, with its imposing homes, as it looked about the time Dubois arrived.

Coffee planter R. Boyd, shown here with his Javanese servants and a tiger cub, often entertained the Duboises on his plantation.

A Riverbank Prize: The Remains of the Earliest Man

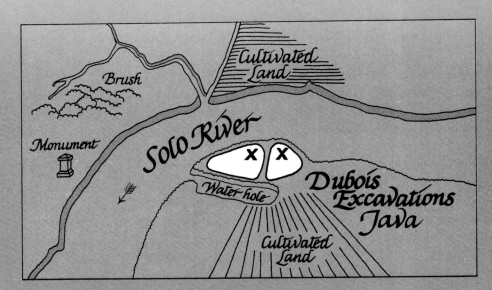

A map, based on a sketch in the Dubois family collection, shows the two sites on the Solo River (crosses) where Dubois found the fossils of Homo erectus and the monument (far left) that was built to mark the event.

At this bend in the river Dubois excavated a stratified embankment (center) where the bones of Java man were found 48 feet down.

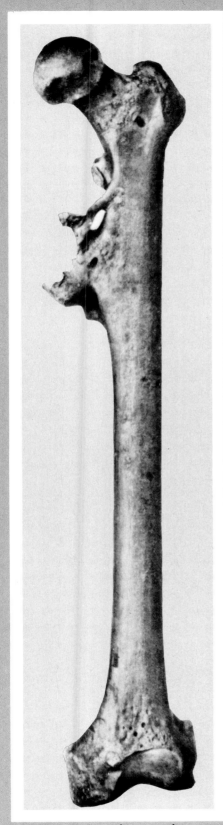

Across the river, Dubois erected a monument with the initials of *Pithecanthropus erectus* (his name for the creature now called *Homo erectus*), a pointer showing the distance to the site, and the years of discovery.

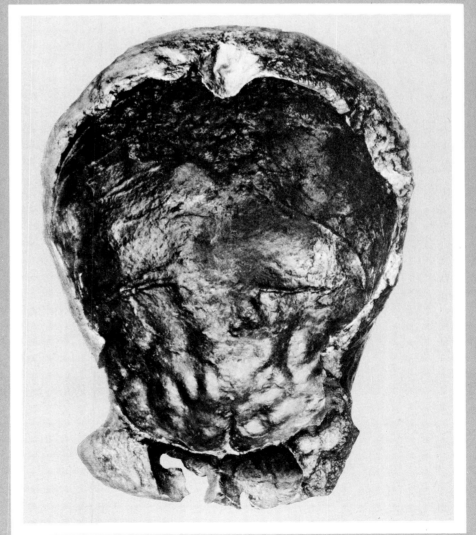

The femur indicated an upright posture.

The stone-encrusted skullcap of Erectus, seen from below, was Dubois' greatest find.

peculiarly hard to place. When digging at the Trinil site began again, starting from the spot where the skull was found, hundreds of skeletons of deer, rhinoceros, stegodon (a primitive elephant), pig, tiger, hyena and crocodile turned up. But it was not until August, 10 months after the apelike skull was found, that another, even more surprising primate fossil was discovered in the same deposit, nearly 50 feet away from the first find. This one was unmistakable: it was the left femur, or thighbone, of a primate that had walked erect! In fact, it resembled a human thighbone in almost every respect, although it was heavier than the thighbone of a modern man. In October, another tooth quite like the first turned up. Could the curious teeth, the troublesome skull and the unexpected thighbone all belong to the same individual?

Together, the four fossils suggested a creature with a skull that was intermediate between ape and man, but with a leg already fully adapted for walking. Such a creature was exactly the sort that a great German scientist, Ernst Heinrich Haeckel, had suggested as a precursor of man. Haeckel had named his hypothetical ancestor *Pithecanthropus,* from the Greek words *pithecos* (ape) and *anthropos* (man). In 1893, seven years after Haeckel had named it, Dubois announced that he had discovered the real Pithecanthropus. To point up the distinctive thighbone, he added the species name *erectus* (upright). He had a monument—a black marble plaque on stone—placed near the spot where Pithecanthropus erectus had been found, and when he dispatched a cable to his friends in Europe announcing the discovery, he confidently said he had found the "Missing Link of Darwin."

As we know today, Pithecanthropus erectus was actually one of the first men, and not a missing link

at all. It is now known to belong to the species Homo erectus, and Dubois' specimen is called Java man. The bones were one of the greatest fossil finds ever made, and Dubois fully realized their immense importance even though he continued to identify them wrongly. While the scientist was traveling home from Java with his wife and children in 1895, a storm at sea sent him scurrying down into the ship's hold, clutching a box containing the fossils. "If something happens," he called to his wife, "you're to take care of the children. I've got to look after this."

But before Dubois could show his discoveries to colleagues in Europe, his precious fossils became the focus of a raging scientific controversy that embroiled him throughout the rest of his life.

His first cabled reports were met with skepticism. Some critics insisted that the fossil bones did not belong together at all and suggested that Dubois had simply made the mistake of mixing the skull and teeth of an ape with the thighbone of a man who had died nearby. One member of the Netherlands Zoological Society, writing in a Dutch newspaper in 1893, ridiculed Dubois' jigsaw-puzzle methods, asking whether more finds at the site in Java might not eventually lead to announcements of an even stranger creature. If a right thighbone more like an ape's should turn up, wouldn't this make Pithecanthropus lopsided? Or if another left thighbone was found, must Pithecanthropus be said to have two left legs? Or, if another, more human skull was discovered within 50 feet of the other bones, would this mean that Pithecanthropus had two skulls, one apelike and one manlike?

The arrival of the fossils themselves for close inspection did not settle the arguments. Only six weeks after Dubois reached Holland in 1895, he presented

Pithecanthropus to the Third International Congress of Zoology at Leiden. Almost at once, a great quarrel broke out over where to place this Java "ape-man" in the scheme of evolution. Opinion seemed to harden along national lines; most Germans believed that Pithecanthropus was an ape that had manlike characteristics; most Britons thought it was a man that had apelike attributes; and the Americans tended to lean toward a transitional form more along the lines Dubois had suggested.

Soon afterward, Dubois carried the bones to London, where he displayed them in the lecture room of the British Zoological Society. Given this chance for a closer look, the British scientists became even more convinced that Pithecanthropus was a primitive man and not the missing link Dubois supposed it. Sir Arthur Keith, one of the leading anthropologists of his day, later described Dubois' undisguised reaction at that meeting: "Dubois was politely impatient with his critics; he attributed their opposition to ignorance or to personal animosity, rather than to a desire to reach the truth."

To garner support for his opinions, Dubois showed his fossils to any scientist who wanted to examine them. Many scientists of the day visited Dubois in Holland, and Dubois traveled widely to show off the bones, carrying them about in a battered suitcase. After a while, he seemed to develop an almost personal attachment to the fossil ancestor who was by now a constant companion. His affection for the over-half-a-million-year-old bones was demonstrated one day in Paris, where he had gone to show Pithecanthropus to a leading French anthropologist, Leonce Pierre Manouvrier. The two men met in the Parisian's anthropology laboratory and discussed the bones until almost midnight. Finally, Dubois mentioned that he was hungry, and they left for dinner in a small, quiet restaurant nearby. Dubois took the fossils, carrying them in the old suitcase. In the restaurant, the two men talked until a waiter told them it was closing time and asked them to leave. Then, Manouvrier later related, he insisted that he accompany Dubois to his hotel to continue their talk. They crossed the street, still heavy with traffic despite the late hour, and had gone several blocks when Dubois grabbed Manouvrier by the arm and cried out, "Where is Pithecanthropus? I've left him in the restaurant!"

Dubois darted back to the restaurant, dashing through the traffic and arriving just as the proprietor was locking up. "Where is Pithecanthropus?" the Dutchman demanded as he caught his breath. No one knew what he was talking about, but the waiter said he had found an old valise and had put it behind the counter. Dubois brushed past him and fell upon the suitcase, opening it quickly to assure himself that Pithecanthropus was still there. That night, Manouvrier told Dubois, he had better put Pithecanthropus under his pillow.

As Dubois carted his fossil bones about to scientific meetings and published detailed descriptions in learned journals, the controversy only increased. By 1928 a summary of scientific opinion listed 15 different interpretations of the fossils. Some views were based on anatomical hairsplitting, others on cruder reasoning. One author, interested in an abnormal thighbone spur that suggested a trace of bone disease, concluded Pithecanthropus must have been a man because an ape could not limp through life as easily as a man. Pithecanthropus, he suggested, might have been supported by his family!

A Career Rewarded with Fame, Marred by Dispute

When Dubois returned to the Netherlands from Java in 1895, news of his discovery of Java man had already made him renowned in scientific circles. He traveled widely, lecturing and displaying his fossils, and in 1898 resumed his academic career at the University of Amsterdam.

But continuing disputes over the meaning of his finds eventually embittered him. He insisted that Java man was a missing link between man and ape rather than human, as many other experts thought. When his views were not accepted, he withdrew to his home in Haarlem and saw few visitors until a few years before his death in 1940.

Dubois' Java man model holds an antler.

Dubois withdrew to this Haarlem house.

At Teyler's Museum, beside the Spaarne River, Dubois was curator of the paleontological collection. He kept his own fossils in a safe.

Dubois' own village, Eijsden, named a street after him in 1952.

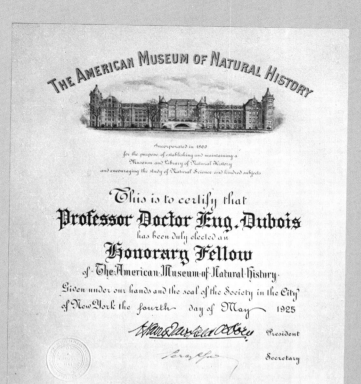

The U.S. honored Dubois with this prized museum fellowship.

At age 80, Dubois (center) and Dutch colleagues were visited in Leiden by Franz Weidenreich (left), famed for work on Peking man.

For many years, Dubois made every effort to give his colleagues as much detailed knowledge of Pithecanthropus as he could. He had to acquire the skills of a dentist, photographer and sculptor in the process. In order to make accurate brain casts, he spent weeks learning to use a fine dental drill, with which he could clean away minute stone particles inside the skullcap. He invented a special "stereorthoscope" camera, designed to photograph the fossils in various planes without distortion. And for the public he sculpted a life-sized reconstruction of Pithecanthropus, ordering his son to pose for him during a school vacation. The statue *(page 46)* was exhibited at the International Exposition in Paris in 1900 and later installed in the Leiden museum, where it is now known affectionately as Pete.

But the attacks on Pithecanthropus continued. Dubois took them all personally. Deeply hurt by the fact that other scientists would not accept his interpretation of the fossil bones, he finally withdrew the fossils from further examination and study, and became almost a recluse himself. Rumor had it that he buried the precious fossils under the floor boards of his house. It was also said, by church-minded critics who considered the theory of evolution sacrilege, that Dubois was at last repenting for his great sin, Pithecanthropus. Finally, after more than 30 years of refusing to see any scientific visitors, Dubois relented and in 1932 invited several prominent anthropologists to his home. Pithecanthropus, a newspaper correspondent reported, had come out of retirement.

Even then, Dubois remained at odds with the scientific community. To the end he insisted that Pithecanthropus was the missing link, while a younger generation of anthropologists was coming to general agreement that Pithecanthropus was the Java representative of the earliest man, Homo erectus.

Today there still remain some unanswered questions about Dubois' discovery. Did the bones really belong together? To suppose that two different primates—an unknown species of ape and an unknown species of man—had both lived in Java at exactly the same time, and had died within 50 feet of each other at Trinil, seemed to Dubois far more improbable than to suppose that the various bones belonged to one creature with both apelike and human characteristics. But scientists are still arguing the point. The skull is unquestionably that of an early man, but one tooth at least may have belonged to a prehistoric orangutan, and some experts suspect that the thighbone came from a higher stratum and belonged to a more modern form of man.

Because of the great controversy over whether Pithecanthropus was a man, an ape or a missing link, Dubois' brilliant detective work in locating the fossils only seemed to add to the mystery of man's origins instead of solving it. But while anthropologists argued over the bones of Java man and Dubois withdrew into his home in Holland, the controversy was being settled elsewhere.

On October 21, 1907, a new clue to man's past turned up in Germany. On that day, two workmen were digging in a huge commercial sand pit near Mauer. Several fossils had previously turned up there, and geologists from Heidelberg University had asked the owner of the pit to save any bones that were found, particularly anything that looked human. This day, digging nearly 80 feet down below ground level, one of the workmen struck a large jawbone with his shovel and split it in half. The jaw looked human, but it seemed much too large to belong to a man. The workmen took it to the owner, who quickly notified Professor Otto Schoetensack at the university. The professor rushed out to Mauer and took possession of the jaw, which he cleaned, repaired and studied with growing excitement. The fossil was so wide and thick that, without its teeth, it might easily have been mistaken for the jaw of a large ape. But the teeth were unmistakably human, and remarkably like the teeth of modern man. They had bigger roots and were slightly larger than our teeth, but they showed all the characteristics that distinguish modern man's teeth from those of the ape, including small canines and molars worn flat by chewing. In a monograph describing the find, Schoetensack created a new species of man on the basis of this one lower jaw —*Homo heidelbergensis,* or Heidelberg man. Today it is considered simply a European example of the widespread Homo erectus species.

From the jaw alone, it was impossible to tell very much about what Heidelberg man looked like. Much more revealing was the place where Heidelberg man turned up. The fossil jaw was found in amongst strata of rock where other extinct animal fossils were also found. Because the era when these animals had lived was known, the Heidelberg jaw could be dated: It belonged to someone who lived about 500,000 years ago. This great age was of significance, the first hint that man had come so far north, into the wintry climates of Europe, at so early a date.

Despite the importance of the jaw, it was too small a piece of evidence to throw much light on Heidelberg man's ancestry. And it was nearly two decades before another fossil like it was found, this time in Peking and only after a painstaking and systematic search. In fact, the discovery of Peking man in 1927 involved a piece of scientific detective work almost as remarkable as Dubois' exploit in Java.

Peking man was added to man's family tree simply because a small band of scientists had gone to China determined to hunt him down. Even after Dubois' success in Java, the prospect of searching for primitive man in China could appeal only to men who were prepared to spend their lives hunting for a needle in one haystack after another. But a Swedish geologist, John Gunnar Andersson, and a Canadian anatomist, Dr. Davidson Black, were sure that a human ancestor would turn up in China if only they looked long and hard enough.

Their belief was based on geologic evidence showing that the ancient climate and geography of China were quite suitable for a primitive man's existence there, and on a theory that patterns of evolution were closely related to climatic conditions. But there was also a single, tantalizing piece of fossil evidence that some early primate had once inhabited China.

In 1899 a European doctor had chanced upon an unusual fossil tooth among some dragon's bones that were about to be ground up for medicine in a druggist's shop in Peking. The tooth was among more than a hundred dragon's bones the doctor picked up in various Chinese drugstores and sent to Max Schlosser at the University of Munich. Schlosser identified the tooth as "a left upper third molar, either of a man or a hitherto unknown anthropoid ape" and predicted hopefully that a further search might turn up the skeleton of an early man.

It was not until 1921 that the search actually began. That year a group led by John Gunnar Andersson

In caves in Dragon Bone Hill near Choukoutien, scientists dug for early man in 1921.

A grid painted on rock enables diggers to keep a record of the locations of their finds.

High on Dragon Bone Hill, workers stand above an ancient cave where digging began.

Deep in the hill, the cave floor is seen.

began to dig at a site 25 miles southwest of Peking, near the village of Choukoutien. Excavations were proceeding at the place—a rise called Chicken Bone Hill near an old limestone quarry—when Andersson overheard his workmen express surprise that he was digging there. There were much better fossils on the other side of the village, the workmen said, at Dragon Bone Hill beside another abandoned quarry. Andersson took the tip and moved to Dragon Bone Hill, where he quickly spotted evidence that his workers had given him good advice. There were bits of broken quartz among the limestone deposits around an ancient cliffside cave. The quartz would not naturally turn up in limestone, Andersson knew. It must have been brought there—perhaps by some toolmaking man of the past. Andersson laid his hand on the limestone cliff and said, "I have a feeling that there lies here the remains of one of our ancestors and it's only a question of finding him."

A great many fossils were dug out of the rock and shipped back to Sweden for study. Twenty different mammals were identified, many of them extinct species, but Andersson's ancestor was not so easily found. A tooth turned up—but it was mistaken for the molar of an ape. Finally in 1926, when one of Andersson's associates had given up and returned to Sweden and the digging had stopped, a closer study of this molar and another tooth found later suggested that they were in fact human.

The teeth were sent back to Andersson, who now turned them over to Dr. Davidson Black, head of the anatomy department of the Peking Union Medical College, for his expert appraisal. Black had come to Peking in 1919, to join the staff of the college then being set up with Rockefeller Foundation funds. He firmly believed that primitive man would one day be discovered in China and he had taken the post in Peking hoping to find some time for fossil hunting there. But after an early inspection tour of the burgeoning college, an advisor from the Rockefeller Foundation had warned Black not to spend too much time on anthropology: "If you think of anatomy for nine months out of the year," he wrote, "it is no one's business what you do with the other three months in the summer. But for the next two years at least, give your entire attention to anatomy."

Setting up an anatomy department in Peking did keep Black busy during his first years there and left him little time to search for primitive ancestors. One of his many problems was getting the cadavers his students needed for dissection. Because even the poorest Chinese worshipped their ancestors, no one in Peking was willing to let a deceased relative be turned over to the school. Black appealed to the governor of a local prison for assistance. Shortly afterwards, the governor sent three bodies—headless. When he was informed that anatomy students needed their cadavers intact, the governor forthwith sent a group of condemned prisoners marching over. With them came a note addressed to Black saying, "Kill them any way you like."

Preoccupied though Black was with medicine, he never lost interest in the Choukoutien digs. And he became deeply involved when Andersson, preparing to return home for a leave, gave him the teeth from Choukoutien. Black persuaded his friends in the Rockefeller Foundation to support a large-scale excavation of the site, and work soon resumed. On October 16, 1927, another tooth was unearthed. Without waiting for any further proof, Black boldly announced the discovery of a new genus and species of prehistoric man, *Sinanthropus pekinensis*.

Scientists were startled, and many refused to recognize Peking man as a legitimate ancestor on the evidence of only a few teeth. But Black, about to begin a furlough from Peking, went on a world tour with the most recent find. As he visited his colleagues around the world, he let them examine the evidence for themselves, casually taking the newly found tooth from a small screw-topped brass capsule he kept fastened to his watch chain.

Then, when he returned to Peking in 1928, Black's belief in the antiquity of Sinanthropus was vindicated. His associates were waiting with fragments of a primitive human jaw they had dug out of the cave. The next year, a Chinese paleontologist working with Black, W. C. Pei, turned up the first skull of Sinanthropus. After removing it from the cave, Pei carefully wrapped it up, set it in the basket of his bicycle and cautiously pedaled the 25 miles to Black's laboratory in Peking. The skull, together with the jaw and teeth, provided a clear picture of Peking man. He seemed to resemble Java man and Heidelberg man, although it was to be many years before scientists agreed that he, like the others, was not a unique species but a type of Homo erectus. Excavations at Choukoutien went on for almost 10 more years, finally taking on the proportions of a grandiose engineering project. The excavations established the humble cave as one of the most important of all Homo erectus sites.

As work advanced at Choukoutien a whole hillside was sliced off, revealing deposits 170 feet deep —about as far down as a 17-story apartment building goes up. A total of 1,873 workdays were devoted to dynamiting and removing some 20,000 cubic meters of rock and earth and sorting through the debris for fossils. The findings comprised an encyclopedia of prehistory, from which a great part of our knowledge of the first men has come. The most important treasures were the human fossils. By 1937 parts of more than 40 men, women and children had been unearthed. These fossils included 5 skulls, 9 skull fragments, 6 facial fragments, 14 lower jaws and 152 teeth. Several connected caves were eventually explored, and in the largest one 100,000 stone tools and fragments (mostly quartz) were found, along with 10 layers of hearths. The charcoal in some of the hearths was 22 feet deep—dramatic evidence that the first men did not permit their fires to die out. There was also an impressive collection of tools fashioned from animal bones and antlers.

Black did not live to see this work completed. He died on March 15, 1933, but he saw enough of the excavation to realize its extraordinary significance. His successor at Choukoutien was Dr. Franz Weidenreich, a German anatomist who reached Peking in 1935. After his arrival, only two more seasons of undisturbed digging were carried out—then the archeologists had to take refuge from bands of skirmishing soldiers, as fighting between Chinese and Japanese guerrillas broke out near Choukoutien. With the approach of World War II, Weidenreich concentrated on making accurate drawings and casts of the Peking skulls and publishing detailed photographs and descriptions of every important fossil.

While Weidenreich and his colleagues were consolidating what they knew about Peking man, news came from Java that a new set of Pithecanthropus fossils had turned up, not far from where Dubois had

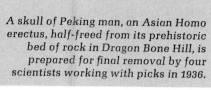

A skull of Peking man, an Asian Homo erectus, half-freed from its prehistoric bed of rock in Dragon Bone Hill, is prepared for final removal by four scientists working with picks in 1936.

Chinese workers carry rock fragments from the cave site for sifting; behind them, numbered squares identify fossil-bearing layers.

found the original specimen almost 40 years earlier. Between 1937 and 1941, Gustav Heinrich Ralph von Koenigswald excavated in the area and discovered, among other important finds, five skull fragments that were definitely human and definitely very old—presumably remains of the same type of Java man that Dubois had found 40 years before.

In 1939 a historic meeting of Peking man and Java man took place in Weidenreich's laboratory, when Von Koenigswald paid a visit and brought his fossils along. Von Koenigswald described this unique occasion in a later memoir: "We laid out our finds on the large table in Weidenreich's modern laboratory: on the one side the Chinese, on the other the Javanese skulls. The former were bright yellow and not nearly so strongly fossilized as our Javanese material; this is no doubt partly owing to the fact that they were much better protected in their cave than the Pithecanthropus finds, which had been embedded in sandstone and tufa. Every detail of the originals was compared: in every respect they showed a considerable degree of correspondence." The two scientists concluded that Pithecanthropus and Sinanthropus were indeed close relations.

In this conclusion, they were bitterly opposed by the aging Eugène Dubois. Dubois continued to insist that his own find was quite distinct from all others, but Von Koenigswald and Weidenreich were little disturbed by the distant thunder of Dubois' protests. Far more disturbing was the rumble of the thundering guns of war.

When the Japanese occupied Java in 1942, they demanded that Von Koenigswald give up his fossils. He did surrender a few, but he also substituted cleverly faked plaster casts for some of the originals. The real fossils he gave for safekeeping to a Swiss geologist and a Swedish journalist—neutrals in the conflict between Allies and Axis (the journalist put the teeth in milk bottles and buried them one night in his garden). Von Koenigswald himself was interned; but when he was released from prison camp after the war, he easily tracked down and reassembled all of the fossils except one—a skull sent to Japan as a birthday present to the emperor. Von Koenigswald filed a report on this loss, and eventually it reached anthropologist Walter Fairservis—then a young lieutenant serving under General Douglas MacArthur in the military government in occupied Japan. Fairservis promptly found the skull in the emperor's Household Museum. Von Koenigswald had in the meantime gone to America. As he later wrote: "One day, when I was working in New York, a young officer appeared unexpectedly and with a polite bow handed me back the skull."

Not so fortunate as Java man was Peking man. He did not survive the war, although Weidenreich escaped to America with his excellent drawings and plaster casts of the fossil skulls. Before the Japanese reached Peking, there was a great debate among the scientists studying Sinanthropus over what to do with the fossils. They actually belonged to the Geological Survey of China, and many people felt they should remain in China, hidden away somewhere in Peking or in the provinces. At last, the Chinese scientists themselves decided to ship the fossils to America for safekeeping.

Packed off to the U.S. Embassy, the boxes of fossils were entrusted to a detachment of Marines as they evacuated Peking. Nine Marines, with their baggage and Peking man, went by special train to the port of Chinwangtao, where the steamship *President Harrison* was waiting for them. Somewhere between the Peking depot and the *President Harrison,* the boxes of fossils disappeared. The ship was grounded by its own crew to prevent its capture and use by the Japanese; the Marines were captured and brought back to Peking as prisoners.

But the boxes with the bones of Peking man vanished without a trace. They have never been found, despite the detective work of countless investigators who continue to try to track down every clue to their fate. Shortly after the Marines were captured, Japanese officers made a painstaking search of the Peking Union Medical College looking for the fossils. They did not know what happened to them, although the officers took several of Peking man's stone tools and some of Davidson Black's original notebooks to Tokyo. The precious boxes may have been aboard a lighter that capsized in the harbor on the way out to the *President Harrison.* Or they may have found their way into the hands of local Chinese druggists, who ground them up as dragon's bones.

In the 1950s the new Communist government of China accused the United States of hiding the missing fossils at the American Museum of Natural History in New York—a charge that was later traced to a garbled report of a meeting between a British anthropologist and Weidenreich at the museum in the postwar years. Apparently, the British anthropologist was shown a cast of the Peking skull by Weidenreich, but when he later told of seeing it he failed to make clear that it was only a cast. A student who heard the story in England later went to China and reported that the original skull was in New York.

In 1971 a New York physician claimed that he was the last to see the boxes and that he had hidden the fossils in the homes of Chinese friends and in warehouses before he was taken prisoner by the Japanese. The search goes on. It seems that Peking man, after lying buried at Choukoutien for nearly half a million years, reappeared for only 12 short years before disappearing again, perhaps forever.

By the time anthropologists were able to resume the search for early man after World War II, the ancestry of man had been traced to forebears more primitive and apelike than Java man. In 1924, Raymond Dart had turned up in Africa fossils of the creature he called *Australopithecus,* which seemed to be an ancient but remarkably manlike ape. Yet there was still no clear conception of man's lineage, or the relationships between the various fossils found in different parts of the world. Had man's body evolved toward its modern form more rapidly than his brain, or had the brain outstripped the body in early human evolution? Were there many different species of early man, evolving at different rates and in different ways in various parts of the world? Or was there a single, consistent pattern governing man's worldwide evolution? In part, these crucial questions could not yet be answered because the answer was obscured by the most peculiar human fossils of all—the skull and jawbone of a creature known as Piltdown man.

When they turned up in a gravel pit on an old farm in Sussex, England, in 1911, these fossils were seen as an important new clue to man's past. The discoverer of Piltdown man was an amateur archeologist named Charles Dawson. He reported that while taking a walk near a place called Piltdown Common, he spotted unusual brown flints being used to mend the road. He asked where they had come from and was led to a nearby farm where workmen were digging gravel. The pit looked to him like a possible source of fossils, and he asked the men to save any they found; on his later visits to the farm he retrieved several parts of a seemingly ancient human skull. He told his story and showed the fossils to A. Smith Woodward of the British Museum, and together they made an exhaustive search of the gravel pit. Many fragments of the skull were found—apparently smashed and scattered by the workmen—as well as half a slightly damaged jaw. On December 18, 1912, the two men introduced Piltdown man to the members of the Geological Society of London. Smith Woodward formally named this creature *Eoanthropus dawsoni*, or Dawson's dawn man.

At first sight, Piltdown man was a complete surprise. He had the skull of a modern man—an imposing brain case and a vertical forehead with slightly ridged brows. But he also had the primitive jaw of an ape. It was almost exactly like a chimpanzee's jaw except that the molars were ground down, the way a man's teeth are worn by chewing. Unfortunately, a small section of the jaw that could have proved whether it fit the skull, a point of attachment called the condyle, had been broken off.

Piltdown man was so strange that astonished anthropologists were forced to revise completely their ideas about evolution. The small brain case and manlike thighbone of Java man had suggested that man's body had evolved more rapidly than his brain. Piltdown man suggested the opposite: that the brain had evolved first. Just as some scientists doubted that the different parts of Java man belonged together, there were skeptics who felt that the Piltdown skull did not go with the jaw. But a great many of the world's leading experts welcomed Piltdown man into the family of human ancestors.

Then, over the years, troubling discrepancies were noted in the Piltdown fragments. The maturity of different parts seemed to vary, and one expert complained that Piltdown man was not only man-brained and ape-jawed, but appeared to have a middle-aged skull, a young jaw and an elderly set of teeth! But the downfall of Piltdown man did not come until the 1950s, when so many genuine fossils of early man and his ancestors had been found that Dawson's discovery stood out like a transistor radio in a collection of stone hand axes. All the other fossils confirmed that man's brain had evolved toward its modern form somewhat more slowly than the rest of his physical equipment. Thus Piltdown man was an evolutionary freak—or could it be a fraud?

The first scientist to test the latter idea was J. S. Weiner, a lecturer in Oxford University's anatomy department, then headed by the famed anatomist Sir Wilfred Le Gros Clark. Weiner tried out his suspicions of Piltdown man on Le Gros Clark, who doubted at first that the fossils could be fraudulent. Then Weiner took a chimpanzee jaw from the anatomy department collection, filed down the teeth to resemble those of Piltdown man and stained his handiwork to make it look like a fossil. Placing the jaw on Le Gros Clark's desk, he said he had found it in the anatomy collection and asked what it could be. The resemblance to the Piltdown jaw was remarkable. Convinced now that Weiner must be right, Le Gros Clark joined him in initiating a thorough reexamination of Dawson's discovery.

Lately devised tests that could tell how old a fossil was by how much fluorine it had absorbed from the earth showed the Piltdown jaw to be quite modern, and when a magnifying glass was used on the teeth, file marks showed up clearly. In 1953 Weiner and Le Gros Clark announced that the jaw was a hoax. The British humor magazine *Punch* met this news with a cartoon—it showed Piltdown man sitting in a dentist's chair, with the dentist saying: "This may hurt, but I'm afraid I'll have to remove the whole jaw."

After further tests, the rest of Piltdown proved to be fraudulent as well. Fragments of several different modern skulls, along with the expertly hoked-up orangutan's jaw (and a few genuinely ancient animal bones to suggest the age of the deposit), had all been planted in the gravel bed. Who put them there, and why, has never been proved, but the circumstances suggest that Dawson could have done it. As an amateur archeologist, he had certainly acquired the knowledge and the skill to have carried out such a hoax. He died in 1916, thirty-seven years before the forgery was finally detected.

Whoever did contrive the Piltdown hoax went to great pains to carry it out. All the fragments were antiqued with potassium dichromate, a chemical that gave them the dark brown color of fossils. The forger, besides filing down the teeth and knocking off the telltale condyle joint of the jaw—which would have revealed that the jaw did not match the skull—had also removed the canine tooth, which is long and pointed in an orangutan's jaw. (Soon after Dawson announced his discovery of Piltdown man, Smith Woodward, the British anthropologist to whom Dawson had first taken the bones, made a model of what he thought Piltdown man's canine ought to look like.

Later, a worn-down canine tooth that was almost exactly like the model "turned up" when Dawson revisited the gravel bed.)

Once the Piltdown puzzle was disposed of, scientists began to perceive the basic pattern of man's evolution from the prehistoric apes. Java man and Peking man, and many more recent finds in other parts of the world, all fell into place. A great many new fossils and living sites of the first men have been discovered in recent decades. Almost as important as the new finds, however, is the fact that scientists have arrived at a far better understanding of what these fossils signify. As improved methods of dating were devised, and a clear scheme of classification developed, it became possible to see the first men, with all their differences in anatomical detail, evolving together as a single species, *Homo erectus,* spread over many parts of the world.

In 1955 several jaws and part of a skull were discovered in a sand pit in Ternifine, Algeria, showing that Homo erectus had once inhabited North Africa. In 1960 a Homo erectus skull turned up in East Africa in the rich layers of fossil deposits at Olduvai Gorge in Tanzania, where Louis and Mary Leakey had already found the bones and tools of his ancestor, Australopithecus. Three years later, human fossils somewhat older and more primitive than those of Peking man were discovered in China, near the town of Lantien, 600 miles southwest of Peking. In 1965 a quarry in Vértesszöllös, Hungary, 30 miles from Budapest, yielded a Homo erectus skull more recent and larger brained than any discovered earlier.

As all these fossils were compared and studied, it became apparent that there were some broad similarities among them; allowing for the fact that they came from such widely scattered places, and that they might differ in age by as much as a million years, the similarities seemed much more striking than the individual variation. Once the classifiers recognized this fact they were able to clear up the confusion caused by the initial naming of the fossils, each with its own separate genus and species. Names like *Pithecanthropus* and *Sinanthropus* were discarded. *Homo erectus* encompassed them all. The great wave of discoveries in recent years has simply demonstrated the wide range of living sites and physical characteristics of the classic Homo erectus type, and shown that over the million years of his existence he slowly evolved from an apelike form indistinguishable from Australopithecus to a human form indistinguishable from Homo sapiens. The skull found at Vértesszöllös, Hungary, for example, borders on the modern, while the skull from Lantien, China, is almost too primitive to be put with the rest.

In the search for the first men, much of the initial excitement over the discoveries of the fossil hunters centered around the skulls of human ancestors. Along the way, however, scientists have accumulated a vast store of other fossils—tools and artifacts the first men made and used, such as those unearthed in Choukoutien. At some sites, like Terra Amata in France and Torralba in Spain, no human bones were found but the artifacts told much about the men who used them. No fossil bones of Homo erectus have been discovered yet in India or the Middle East, but tools like those he used elsewhere have been found, and he is assumed to have lived there as well.

In some places, such as Vértesszöllös, the combination of human bones and artifacts has seemed a puzzle. The fossils found here, for example, suggest that their owners were highly advanced for Homo erectus, and yet, mysteriously, they used more primitive types of tools than their smaller-brained contemporaries in other parts of the world. So long as any such puzzles and questions remain, the fossil hunters will go on hunting. But the search has already provided an enormous amount of information about the first men and their great inventions of fire, organized hunting, language and family life—the cultural heritage that, far more than any physical distinction, was to set man apart from his fellow inhabitants of the planet.

Terra Amata: Homo Erectus on the Riviera

One of the most revealing of all Homo erectus finds, rich in details about his skills and habits, has helped to fill in the fragmentary portrait of the first man sketched by earlier archeologists. It turned up in 1966 in the busy Mediterranean city of Nice, in the heart of the French Riviera.

The story of the discovery begins in October 1965, when a construction site near the cliff road to Monte Carlo attracted an unusually knowledgeable sidewalk superintendent: a short, dark-eyed official prehistorian of Marseilles, 30-year-old Henry de Lumley. He could not be sure that the bulldozers tearing into the shoulder of Mount Boron would turn up anything of interest but he was not about to let them sweep away the past without having a look. His interest in the site had been whetted eight years before when laborers, preparing the ground for new apartments, uncovered a stone tool and a few flint flakes. At that time, the contractor went broke before the work could go much further, and the operations ceased. But then, in 1965, a new contractor announced his intention of constructing a five-story luxury apartment house on the same spot.

The site is a choice location: just above it on sloping ground stands the handsome Château de Rosemont (above), once the residence of a king of Yugoslavia and now being turned into a museum of paleontology by the

The Terra Amata site of Homo erectus camps, first exposed by bulldozers excavating the land for an apartment house, lies on a hill below the Château de Rosemont in Nice.

city of Nice; just a few blocks down is the commercial port of Nice and nearby is an alley called Terra Amata —"beloved land" in the local dialect. (Originally it had been known as Terra Mata—"crazy land"—but this name apparently had offended the nearby residents' sense of propriety, and it accordingly was changed.)

When the new contractor's bulldozers set to work, De Lumley, a specialist in Paleolithic studies, followed the digging like a hawk waiting for a plow to turn a mouse from its burrow. His dedication paid off. As a bulldozer

sheared off about three feet of ground, some objects glinted in the sunlight. "Stop!" De Lumley shouted; he had spotted what he quickly recognized as beach pebbles that had been shaped by human hands.

In France, where prehistoric artifacts may crop up anywhere, archeology takes precedence over new construction, and De Lumley knew he could count on the support of the then Minister of Cultural Affairs, André Malraux. The bulldozers backed off, and a few days later De Lumley and his wife, Marie-Antoinette, an arche-

Stretched prone on elevated planks crisscrossing the dig, fossil hunters painstakingly investigate their small territories—each worked on a 39-inch-square section of the site.

ologist, triumphantly nailed to the fence around the project an official notice warning off all trespassers—and construction workers—on pain of fine and imprisonment.

The contractor, confronted by a costly delay, could hardly have been less enthusiastic; he agreed that Terra Amata was an interesting site for archeologists and prehistorians, but, he added sourly, "for us it's of no interest at all. We aren't researchers but demolishers."

Now began a battle against time. De Lumley was granted six weeks to excavate 144 square yards on a ledge, but construction was allowed to resume in the main pit. Plainly the race against the bulldozers was not a job for husband and wife working unaided—or even for the usual small team of archeologists. It called for a massive effort. Before long, more than 300 archeologists, students and interested amateurs were involved—climbing to the site each day via a series of ladders and working under a protective canvas. The original time limit was ex-

A digger squeezes into a crevice excavated between two Paleolithic beaches. The upper level is the sandy beach on which the first men built their huts.

tended, and between January 28 and July 5, 1966, this army of diggers, equipped with everything from bulldozers to trowels, quickly dug down almost 50 feet, cutting through hundreds of thousands of years of geologic history, before they finally uncovered an ancient beach that bore traces of human habitation.

Then the fossil hunters, using modern methods of excavation (*pages 87-95*) developed to ensure the discovery of every scrap of evidence of ancient man's tenure on the site, spent each day, sunrise to sunset, lying on planks set every which way across the dig. Cautiously and methodically pecking away with their delicate tools —knives, brushes, surgical instruments—they gently dusted whatever they found and poured the sand into oilcans for sifting later.

This meticulous work took the diggers down through a richly rewarding layer of Paleolithic sediment eight feet thick, after which they went down another sixteen feet without finding any further sign of man. In the end, they had sliced vertically through more than 70 feet of the Terra Amata hill.

While inching down through the eight feet of pay dirt, each digger worked on a small area. The site had been divided into sections a meter (39 inches) square, marked off by strings tied to stakes around the edges of the excavation. In this way the location of every relic found could be precisely identified, for relative position reveals much about the identity and purpose of a fossil.

Thus the dig was carried out horizontally, layer by layer. As the work proceeded, the excavators recorded in their notebooks the distance from the middle of each find to the left side of its square; the distance from the back of the square (the side closer to the digger) to the object; and the object's orientation in the ground—whether vertical, horizontal or tilted—which gave some idea of the shape of the ground on which the artifacts had been left. Once these notations were made, the diggers drew to scale on graph paper the plans of their particular squares and marked the exact location of each discovery. The sub-

This foot-wide hole is believed to have held posts that propped up Erectus' huts.

An adult human footprint, 400,000 years old, is the most ancient ever discovered.

surrounded by pebbles that someone had placed there to protect the fire from the northwest wind, still the prevailing wind in Nice today. The fact that the hut was such a drafty affair led De Lumley to surmise that it may have been made of saplings or branches. A circular area around the fireplace was free of litter, suggesting that the inhabitants slept there.

Only a few steps away from the hearth, De Lumley uncovered a toolmaker's workshop, in the middle of which was a flat stone. Here, he guessed, the toolmaker had sat; tools and chips lay scattered about the seat. "This stone wasn't naturally on the sandy beach," De Lumley said. "It was clearly carried here to sit on." One of the most interesting finds in the workshop area was a rock that had been shattered and discarded; it could be reassembled from 11 fragments—a 400,000-year-old jigsaw puzzle.

The most dramatic of all the discoveries, however, was a nine-and-a-half-inch footprint made by an adult whose heel slipped slightly as he stepped in the mud. It is the oldest adult human footprint ever found.

If there had been no other discoveries, these alone would have been enough to excite anthropologists everywhere. But the richness of the site exceeded De Lumley's dreams. No fewer than 21 levels of habitation came to light, layered one on top of

sequent juxtaposition of all of the charts, coupled with photographs and casts of the finds, enabled De Lumley to reconstruct the various levels of the ancient habitation.

In five feverish months, De Lumley's team exposed 35,000 objects, whose positions were recorded on 1,200 charts, 9,000 photographs and 108 square yards of casts—one of the most unexpected and valuable archeological treasures ever found in one small area. "It is as if we are reading a book," De Lumley said while the rewarding work of excavation was still in progress. "Each layer is like a page that we read, and as we read, we know the story of early man."

The first page to be read was the 20-by-40-foot floor of a hut. Several holes, about a foot in diameter, suggested that the roof of the structure had been held up from the inside by two or more posts of some sort—perhaps the trunks of dead trees washed up on shore. In the center of the dwelling was a hearth, a fairly compact area of baked and discolored sand partially

On one of the hut floors, a windscreen of stones still shields a shallow hearth (left).

another, and they plainly reveal what the world's oldest known architectural structures had been like.

The huts had stood in three locations: 4 on a sandbar, 6 on the beach itself and 11 on a dune. They had been built over the course of perhaps a century, though the 11 on the dune, not so old as the others and built one on top of the next, had apparently resulted from as many consecutive visits to the cove by the same band.

The dune where the later camps had been built was evidently an ideal spot, protected by a limestone cliff and close to drinking water from a spring nearby. The huts there were all elongated ovals but varied in size, measuring from 26 to 49 feet long and 13 to almost 20 feet wide. Their shape

Large stones still sit side by side just as they did when used to brace hut walls.

could be determined from the bracing stones still standing in a ring around many of the living floors, and by the imprints of a series of stakes or saplings that must have been stuck into the sand very close together all around the edge to form the walls. At the center of the huts lay the hearths —either as shallow pits or with pebbled surfaces—each shielded by its little stone windscreen, which seemed to corroborate De Lumley's original hunch that the structures were drafty, sapling-walled affairs.

The size of the huts suggested to De Lumley that the groups of hunters had been relatively small, some being perhaps no larger than 15 individuals. On this basis he conjectured that the groups were made up only of men, out

In a reconstruction of man's earliest architecture, bracing stones help support the drafty oval hut, made of bent, stripped branches.

on a short hunting foray. This opinion, however, is not shared by most authorities, who point out that it would have been unfeasible for the men to transport—in their arms or on their backs—an appreciable quantity of meat over any great distance to the women and children of the band who had been left behind.

No human bones were found to provide proof for one side or another of this question, but something of the life of the more recent hut dwellers could be visualized through details patiently extracted from the living floors. In a corner of one of the later huts, not far from a hearth, lay a large smooth stone scarred with tiny scratches. To De Lumley's eye those scratches indicated that meat had been cut on the stone with a smaller piece of sharp stone; bones of many different animals were found nearby.

Close to this "kitchen" area De Lumley came upon another unusual find: specimens of fossilized human excrement. (Homo erectus, it seems, was not the most hygienic of men: though, to his credit, a kind of toilet zone does seem to have been set up in the hut.) Analysis of fossil pollen found in the feces indicated the time of year the hut had been built and occupied—late spring or early summer, when certain flowers, among them yellow broom, were in blossom and shed their pollen over everything that the prehistoric campers ate.

It was also a time when many game animals would have been abundant on the flood plain of the Paillon River, not far from the camp site. The presence of game surely can have been no coincidence. The first men were above all hunters, and the Terra Amata bands must have chosen the site in the late spring because the hunting was good there at that time.

Certainly the animal remains found

A fossil of a stag antler, pebbles and tool chips add clutter to the floor of a hut.

throughout the site corroborate that speculation. There were bones from birds, turtles and at least eight kinds of mammals. The hunters did not spurn rabbits and rodents, but they preferred larger, meatier prey. Many bones were those of the young of big game. The most numerous of them came from the red deer, followed in descending order of abundance by the remains of an extinct species of elephant; wild boar; ibex, or wild mountain goat; the extinct Merk's two-horned rhinoceros; and the extinct wild ox. Only the wild boar still lives in the environs of Nice and it is smaller than its forebears.

The visitors obviously concentrated on hunting while at Terra Amata, but they also indulged a taste for seafood. The shells of oysters, limpets and mussels showed that they appreciated such delicacies. The presence of some fishbones and fish vertebrae indicated that these dune campers fished occasionally as well.

The occupants of the earlier huts on the beach and sand bar differed in sev-

eral ways from those who camped on the dune. For whatever reason, they built bigger fires. They seem also to have been less adept as toolmakers. They left behind several examples of their rather crude skill, including such pebble tools as a pick, flaked on one face only, rough bifaces—oval cobbles that had been chipped on two sides of one end—scrapers, cleavers, choppers and projectile points.

The dune dwellers made many of the same kinds of tools as did their neighbors but employed a more advanced technique in manufacturing them—flaking chips off a core and then shaping the chips themselves. They apparently traveled to find proper materials—a projectile point had been fashioned from a kind of volcanic rock found only in the Esterel region, some 30 miles to the west.

In addition, the dune dwellers used tools manufactured from bone as well as stone. One, fashioned from the leg bone of an elephant, had been hammered to a point. Another had been hardened in fire, and the fragment of a third was blunt with use. A fourth tool had a long, sharp end and may have been employed as an awl to pierce hides, perhaps to make clothing. Impressions in the sand around the larger hearth, unmistakably those of animal skins, indicated that Erectus either sat or slept on hides.

The discovery of several pieces of red ocher, worn to a nub, suggested that the first man may also have decorated his body, perhaps even for ceremonial purposes. Then again the red ocher may have had a more practical, even modern-day, application —tribal peoples living in sunny areas today still mix it with fat and use it as a sunburn preventive.

One of the most intriguing finds was a spherical imprint in the sand. Had it been left by a bowl? De Lumley thinks so and believes that the bowl, presumably of wood, would have been used to store water. But he theorizes that the hut dwellers might also have cooked in such a container, filling it first with water and then adding hot stones to raise the water temperature, a method of boiling food followed until recently by the Indians of the Pacific Northwest.

The possibility that Homo erectus had vessels provides rich ground for further speculation. They may well have been used by women and children to gather nuts, berries and seeds, thus facilitating the division of labor that is the hallmark of his society.

The people who built the huts apparently never stayed long in them. De Lumley could determine this fact from the state of the living floors themselves; they had not been compacted down much. Had the hunters been around for more than several days, they would have pounded the ground hard with their feet. Other evidence pointing to the brevity of the stay was provided by stone tools that were a lighter color on top than bottom. The top surfaces had been bleached by the sun, indicating that the huts that could have shaded them must have collapsed soon after the visitors departed.

The dig at Terra Amata was a tour de force of modern archeology. Not only did it reveal uniquely the life of Homo erectus, but it disclosed much about the climate, geography, flora and fauna of his times. The results of studies by paleontologists and geologists, for instance, made it possible to reconstruct the countryside of Nice at the time of the hunter's visits (drawing below). Terra Amata was colder and more humid then, but the view would present some familiar landmarks for the modern Nicois, such as

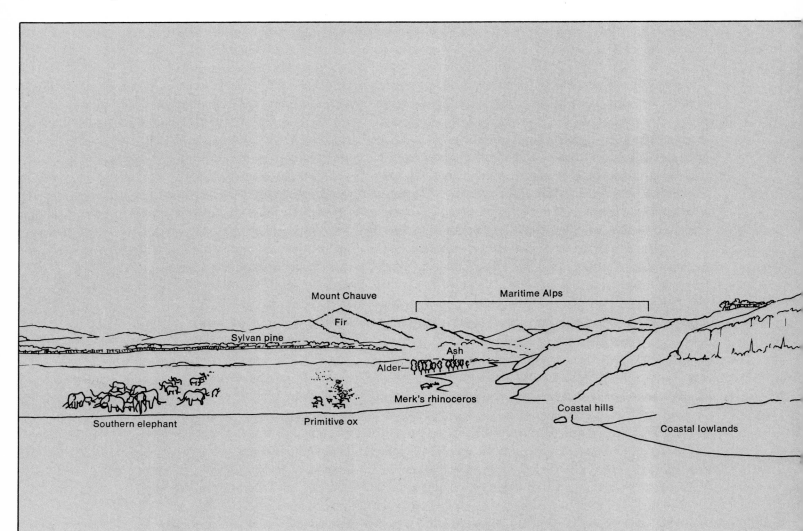

A panorama, drawn by a French artist on De Lumley's staff, suggests how Terra Amata and its environs looked 400,000 years ago. The site, seen here

Mount Chauve in the Alps to the northwest and Mount Boron rising to the east. In fact, the sea had cut a small cave into the western slope of Mount Boron, which provided shelter for the beach of Terra Amata from the north and east wind.

But the Mediterranean was about 85 feet higher then than it is today, and the sea covered most of the plain of Nice and partly filled what is now the Paillon River Valley. That is why Terra Amata, once on the shore of the sea, now overlooks it from a hillside.

There will undoubtedly be other great Homo erectus finds, but Terra Amata exposed the clearest picture yet of the life and times of our first human ancestor. As French historian Camille Jullian has written in summing up the finds revealed there:

' "The hearth is a place for gathering together around a place that warms, that sheds light and gives comfort. The tool-maker's seat is where one carefully pursues a work that is useful to many. The men here may well be nomadic hunters, but before the chase begins, they need periods of preparation and afterwards long moments of repose beside the hearth. The family, the tribe will arise from these customs, and I ask myself if they have not already been born."

Where the hunters of Terra Amata went after their short visits, and why, after visiting the cove for many years, they never came back, are mysteries still. But what has happened to their ancient settlement is no mystery at all. When the last bit of archeological evidence had been lovingly lifted from the ground in July 1966, the bulldozers inexorably closed in. Today, luxury apartments stand where Homo erectus' huts stood more than 400,000 years ago; it is one of the oldest occupied spots in human history.

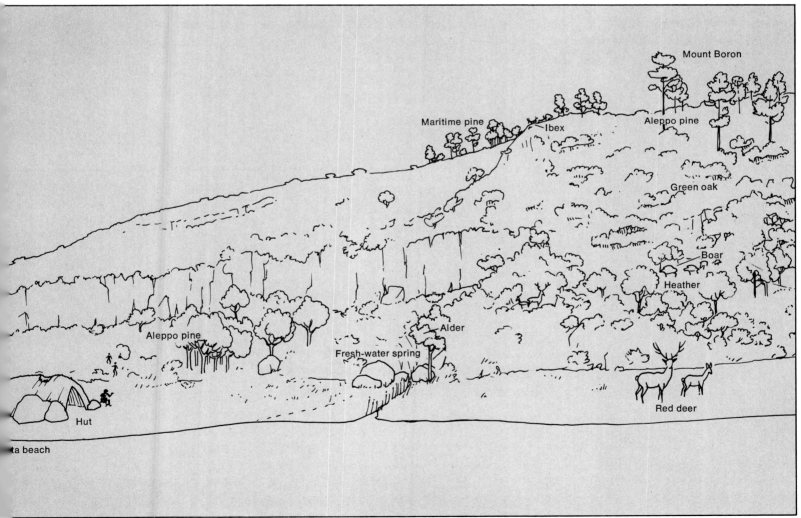

looking north toward the Maritime Alps, was ideal for the early hunters: a sheltered beach with fresh water, game and vegetation near at hand.

Chapter Three: The Hunter

At Olorgesailie in southwestern Kenya archeologists have found dramatic evidence of the success the first men achieved when they took up hunting, a way of life that was to mold the human character until relatively recent times and that was at last to separate man clearly from his primate relatives. The fossil remains at Olorgesailie tell an engrossing story about a creature at work here who was no apelike hominid, but man the hunter.

In an area only 21 yards long and 14 wide, the diggers unearthed bones and teeth of at least 50 adult and 13 juvenile baboons of the now-extinct genus *Simopithecus;* mixed with them were more than a ton of stone tools and cobbles. It was evident that a massive, organized slaughter had been conducted on the site and that the logistics and details of the hunt had to have been worked out well in advance, since both the stones and the tools had been taken to the spot from sources 20 or more miles away. It is easy to reconstruct what must have happened at Olorgesailie a half million years ago.

It is night. Concealed by the darkness a band of hunters steals up on a group of baboons asleep in trees. Having positioned themselves in a circle around the trees, they hurl at their sleeping victims the cobbles they have brought with them. The baboons are big-boned, formidable creatures, the males about the size of a man. They scramble down from the branches, and fight fiercely, their long, sharp ca-

Making a hand ax, the most basic of Homo erectus' tools, a hunter uses a hammerstone to strike a few large flakes from one end of a chunk of quartzite, a rock that fractures to produce a fairly sharp cutting edge. With such implements Homo erectus gained increasing control over his environment and became an ever more efficient killer of large animals.

nines flashing—but teeth are no match for the men's weapons, and when the baboons give up the fight and try to escape, they are clubbed or stoned to death. The hunters proceed to butcher the dead baboons with stone cleavers and hand axes, and in the morning light the attack ends with a feast.

The significant aspect of the Olorgesailie baboon hunt is the logic and efficiency with which it was apparently executed. Men, like other primates, normally sleep by night and are active by day. But in order to take the sleeping baboons by surprise the hunters had to stay awake until a late hour. They had to locate and import the stones for the attack and prepare others beforehand for use as weapons and tools, making an ample stockpile of armaments; and they had to work out a careful battle strategy. In short, there was nothing casual about the hunt—and it must also have taken a great deal of courage to bring off since, presuming it did occur at night, nocturnal predators would have been on the prowl, as eager perhaps to eat the somewhat vulnerable men as the men were to make a meal of the baboons.

By the time of the Olorgesailie baboon ambush, men had already become very skilled hunters. They had taken a long time to reach this level of skill. Long before the first men evolved, hominids hunted. Some nonhuman primates do even today, but in a limited, haphazard way: Chimpanzees seem capable of organizing into hunting parties—but such loose organizations are temporary and infrequent and the chimps are easily distracted from their purpose unless their prey is always in sight or nearby.

The nonhuman primates hunt because they like to eat animal flesh, even though their diet is basically vegetarian. They might even consume meat on a regular basis if they were given the opportunity to do so. When gorillas in captivity are fed meat, they gradually come to prefer it over the leaves, shoots, nuts and roots that are their ordinary fare. At first they may only toy with the meat they are given, but if they keep on sampling it they slowly develop a taste for it, and a change actually occurs in the gorillas' intestines. The ciliate protozoa that digest the cellulose in their normal vegetarian diet gradually disappear and the gorillas begin to develop mammoth carnivorous appetites—the more they eat meat, the more they must have it.

Perhaps a similar hunger developed among the Australopithecines. The fossil evidence shows that they consumed a wide variety of animals, some of which they presumably caught, and some of which they may have scavenged. But they lacked the brain power to be thoroughly consistent hunters, however much they may have relished the variety and excitement that meat brought to their diet.

The picture changed dramatically with Homo erectus. Although he continued to rely heavily on plants for nourishment—as do practically all modern humans—he possessed both the cunning and the tools necessary to assure himself of meat on a fairly regular basis. If hunting had been merely an occasional exercise for his predecessors, it became for the first men a major occupation.

Like all evolutionary change, this crucial development was a slow matter of advantage and capacity reinforcing each other. Man did not go out and become a hunter because some precocious individuals decided they liked meat. But a creature that was able to catch, eat and digest meat was favored, at that time and place, in the competition for survival. Hunting

tremendously increases the human larder, making available far more food per square mile of living space than wild plant life alone can provide. As a vegetarian, man can make use of only a limited number of the things that grow in the ground—mainly roots, nuts, fruits, berries and some tender shoots. The most abundant plants—the grasses of the savanna and the leaves of forest trees—are inedible to humans. But the animals that live on the things that humans cannot digest may themselves be quite edible and, in fact, very nourishing. Thus, previously inedible greens, converted to edible meat, became available through hunting, which, in ecologists' terms, lengthened the food chain. This increase in the usable food supply was a crucial advantage to man because it allowed him to exist in regions, particularly in the temperate zones, which could not have supported him on a vegetable diet alone.

Hunting not only increased the amount of food available to man. It also provided a better food. Meat, particularly when cooked by the fire that our ancestors were slowly learning to tame, was a much more concentrated form of nourishment, a more efficient source of energy than the wild vegetables, fruits and berries that could be foraged. Venison, for instance, yields 572 calories—a measurement of available energy—per 100 grams of weight, while the same weight of most fruits and vegetables yields well under 100 calories. So one medium-sized animal would have provided in a compact, easily carried form the same amount of energy as the results of a whole day's foraging for greens. (Nuts actually yield more calories than most meats and were undoubtedly a vital part of early man's diet when and where he could find them; but they grow only in certain localities and many of them are seasonal, while game is widely available over much longer periods of time.)

Because meat-eating conveyed clear-cut advantages for survival, individuals who had to some small degree the physical or mental traits that made them better hunters were favored in the process of natural selection over those who did not.

The attributes that inched Homo erectus along in his ascendancy as a hunter were not dramatic ones. Most of the basic physical traits that are required for hunting had probably been fully realized earlier in Australopithecus. He walked erect and was a good runner, although Erectus eventually became taller, and thus gained distinct advantages in speed and in height of eye. Similarly, Australopithecus' hands and arms were adapted for fairly accurate throwing, a fundamental hunting skill.

Another major physical change that had already occurred by the time Erectus took on his new role was the adaptation of his skin. When hominids started diverging from the apes and monkeys, they must have been as hairy as those animals are now. Yet as man's ancestors evolved, their hair grew less dense and the sweat glands in their skin multiplied; by the time of Homo erectus the skin had probably become relatively hairless and had developed a complex network of sweat glands. This change sharply differentiated man from other primates: Today, while he still retains as many hair follicles as apes have, his hair is in general much shorter and finer and so undeveloped over large areas of his body as to be almost invisible; conversely, he has two to five million sweat glands, a far greater number than is found in any other primate.

Scientists are not sure why this change in body hair took place, but it seems connected to an increasing ability to sustain strenuous physical exertion—an obvious advantage for a hunter out under the sun through much of the day (by contrast, most carnivores hunt at night). As hominids ancestral to man moved from the protective forests onto the open savanna, they had developed a very high rate of metabolism; that is, their bodies, whether working or resting, burned energy at a faster rate than most animals. This prodigal use of energy means that the body creates a great deal of heat; the efficient cooling system provided by the complex of sweat glands is vital to maintain a safe body temperature.

It seems logical to assume that the evolutionary adaptation to this biological need would have been the development of sweat glands. During heavy exertion or in hot weather these organs bathe the body in moisture that cools the surface, and the blood just below it, as it evaporates. Dense hair would inhibit evaporation of the moisture and would get matted and clogged with dried sweat. Hence, the theory goes, the marked decrease in hair density.

There are, of course, other animals whose natural habitat is the savanna, such as zebras, that sweat heavily during strenuous exertion and yet retain a full coat of hair. But their metabolic rates are noticeably lower than the human one, and they require in general a less efficient heat exchange apparatus because they lead a much less active life.

Sweating is not an unmitigated blessing for humans, though. As William Montagna, professor of dermatology at the University of Oregon, has pointed out, sweating represents "a major biological blunder" in one sense, for it not only drains the body of enormous amounts of moisture requiring that it

A group of Homo erectus hunters attacks and kills a troop of baboons with cobbles in a reconstruction based on fossils found at Olorgesailie. The men, who might have sneaked up on the animals as they slept in trees, carried these naturally rounded missiles (inset) to the site, along with roughly flaked stone tools they fashioned to use in butchering their prey.

have a constant supply of water, but also depletes the system of sodium and other essential elements in its chemical makeup. Montagna suggests that the moisture-producing glands "are still an experiment of nature—demonstrably useful to man but not yet fully refined by the evolutionary process."

In any case, nearly naked, sweating man was certainly better equipped to exert himself for long periods in the tropical sunlight than his ape and monkey relatives were, and it can be assumed that the dramatic changes in his skin, however they occurred, made it possible for him to engage successfully in his new way of life.

If all the important physical adaptations that equipped man for hunting had already been achieved by Erectus' predecessors, what made him so much better a hunter than they were? The answer almost certainly lies in the enormous increase in the size and adaptive capabilities of his brain. Hunting was more than a physical activity; it defined a way of life, involving language, culture and social organization. Hunting became as much a matter of the mind as of the body.

In the first place, with a better brain Erectus had a greater attention and memory span; by being able to retain the information gleaned from his own and his fellows' past hunting experiences, he could amass knowledge of animal behavior, plan ahead, work out strategies and roam farther afield than his forebears without getting lost. His stone tools and weapons were improvements over theirs, and he also had wooden spears, which made hunting safer and more effective. Even if he only jabbed with the spear rather than throw it, he could still attack an animal safely without getting within immediate range of its retal-

iating claws and teeth. And a spear embedded almost anywhere in an animal's body is likely to disable it; a stone, to be equally effective, must be thrown accurately to hit a vulnerable spot.

Perhaps as important as any improvement in weapons technology was a change in tactics. Man gradually advanced enough socially to cooperate with his fellow hunters: he could go out in small bands. The chances of his making kills greatly increased when the jobs of scanning, stalking and slaughtering were shared around. Cooperative tactics brought a major change in strategy; now men in organized groups could take on much larger animals than the Australopithecines had dared to. There was a definite advantage in trying for big game—more meat could be obtained for less time and labor. And it seems reasonable to imagine that even at such an early stage in human development the thrill of the chase stirred a man's blood and the glory and prestige of success in the hunt stoked his ego.

The most striking aspect of Erectus' hunting prowess is that he was able to vanquish animals much bigger and stronger than himself—indeed, he could bring down the largest land animals of his time—with weapons that were literally nothing but sticks and stones. His success must have depended to a large extent on his guile and his understanding of the quarry's behavior. If so, just how did he hunt? Some of his methods are documented in the remains found in excavated sites; others can be inferred by examining hunting techniques employed in modern times by hunter-gatherers. Many of these methods have close parallels in the animal world, and the similarities suggest that early men, faced with the same hunting challenges that confront most social carnivores, responded in the same way.

Lions, for example, often hunt in groups. They use a kind of pincer movement; while two or three advance on their prey from the front, two others approach from the side. Wild dogs always hunt in packs, concentrating on vulnerable young animals. Yapping at a herd of wildebeest, first they try to get the adult males to charge. Then they dash into the center of the herd and harass the mothers and their calves until one of the youngsters panics and flees. Once outside the protective circle of the herd, the animal is doomed. The large number of fossil remains of immature mammals found at Homo erectus sites indicates that the first men had learned well the advantages of picking on the younger, weaker animals as their prey.

If Homo erectus adapted the tactics of other predators to his own ends, he almost certainly did so unconsciously. But his growing brain enabled him to make conscious improvements in hunting methods. Erectus was wise enough to have looked carefully for the weaknesses of the animals he hunted, big or small. The francolin, a bird similar to a partridge that was part of his diet, is still found in Africa and has a survival mechanism that serves it very well except against man. When it sees a predator approach, it flies from the ground and lands a hundred yards or so away. Flushed a second time, the bird once more flutters off—but goes only about half as far. A third time the bird retreats a still shorter distance and then huddles close to the earth motionless; a man with the height of eye to see where it has landed each time, and the wit to figure out the pattern of flight, can follow the francolin and pounce on it.

African hares, though fast on their feet, are equally vulnerable, and they too figured as part of Homo erectus' diet. How easily they can be caught by intelligent man was demonstrated by the late anthropologist Louis Leakey, who ran them down and captured them with his bare hands. The technique is simple. The hunter has only to keep his eyes on the hare's long ears. When the hare is about to dodge, it lays its ears all the way back. Seeing this telltale sign, the hunter veers immediately either to the left or the right—whichever direction he chooses he has a 50-50 chance of picking the way the hare is going to go. If the hunter has guessed correctly he and the animal are now on a collision course, and if he is quick he can scoop up his dinner as it goes by. If he misses, the hare usually will run for cover and freeze there. The hunter, with the advantage of the primate's highly developed color vision, can spot the animal where another predator would be fooled by the hare's camouflage coloring; all the man need do is go over and pick up his prey.

Since Homo erectus could not have run down much of his larger quarry, he probably used a technique that Grover S. Krantz, an anthropologist at Washington State University, has called persistence hunting. Development of this method, too, required insight into the behavior of animals, such as the tendency of ungulates like antelopes and gazelles to move in an arc when trying to escape from a pursuer —giving the hunters the opportunity to cut them off. But the key to persistence hunting is persistence: never allowing the animal to rest, but keeping it constantly in motion until it grows so tired it can go no farther; when it slumps from exhaustion, it can easily be killed. Observers have reported seeing the

Clinging precariously to a horse's mane, an Erectus hunter stabs at his prey with a dagger (inset) fashioned from animal bone. He and his fellows attack the horses as targets of opportunity—the animals are fleeing a fire (background).

Somali hunt Salt's antelope this way. Knowing that the animal cannot tolerate the heat of the midday sun, a hunter drives one from its resting place in the shadow of trees lining a water course. Then, as the antelope trots off to find another cool spot, the hunter follows. "In the course of an hour or so," wrote the 19th Century British explorer J. H. Speke after an African expedition, "the terrified animal, utterly exhausted, rushes from bush to bush, throwing itself down under each in succession until at length it gets captured."

With other less vulnerable animals Homo erectus may have had to keep up the chase for hours on end. The Tarahumara Indians of Mexico have been known to pursue a deer for as long as two days. Although the Indian hunter may at times lose sight of his quarry, he never loses track of its spoor—telltale hoofprints, droppings and other signs of its passage —and relentlessly continues the pursuit until the deer collapses, often, it has been reported, with its hoofs completely worn away.

Stalking can bring down far larger animals than deer. The first men are known to have killed such formidable creatures as ancient elephants, which were considerably bigger than modern species—one such prey stood over 13 feet tall and weighed more than 20 tons. It seems incredible that an animal as huge and tough as an elephant could be killed with nothing but bone and stone weapons and wooden spears. Yet the wooden spear is still used to hunt elephants by Pygmies, whose small size has not left them wanting in bravery. Normally they go out in groups, and when they come across an elephant, one will attack it with his spear. As the animal charges the hunter, the others dash toward it from different angles and

plunge in their spears. They keep this up until the tormented animal dies. Some Pygmies even hunt elephants alone. For this feat the hunter wears no clothing, but smears his body with animal dung to mask his human smell. Once he has located an elephant herd that has paused to rest in the midday heat, he sneaks up on it, and with a favorable wind, stalks one of the beasts. When he is within three or four yards, he rushes forward and spears the animal in the neck. He must beat a quick retreat to escape the thrashings of the wounded elephant. An even more audacious method involves waiting in the bush for a herd to file past. When the last one goes by, the hunter darts between its legs and plunges a lance with a barbed head into its belly. The elephant is unlikely to be killed at once but probably will wander through the jungle, dazed with pain and becoming increasingly weary; the hunter must follow it until it weakens enough so that he can kill it.

If such techniques were indeed used by Homo erectus they must certainly have taken a serious toll of the hunter's energy, and they had the distinct disadvantage of leaving him stranded so far from camp that he could take back only a small part of the animal's flesh. A more productive method would have been the surprise attack by several men, such as the one carried out at Olorgesailie, or an even more elaborate ambush, either of which could slaughter large numbers of animals at one time.

One ambush method that Homo erectus developed and refined was the use of bogs as traps for catching entire herds. At Olduvai Gorge in Africa archeologists unearthed the fossil remains of a herd of pelorovis, an extinct form of cattle. The animals had been driven into a swamp by the hunters and killed as they attempted to free themselves from the mud. The leg bones of one still stood in the clay; the men had apparently hacked away the rest of the carcass and carried it off.

But by far the most dramatic proof that has come down to us of Homo erectus' prowess as a hunter —indeed, one of the most revealing sources of information we have about the first men anywhere —lies on two hillsides above a stream in the Guadarrama mountains of Spain, about 100 miles northeast of Madrid. Called Torralba and Ambrona, the hills face each other across a valley that is the only north-south pass through the mountains for many miles in either direction. Here, preserved in sediment, is evidence that about 400,000 years ago Homo erectus hunters apparently managed to systematically kill a large number of elephants in the course of many seasons. Once again, from the distribution of the bones at the sites and other stray bits of evidence, it is possible to reconstruct what happened—even to imagine in detail what took place during an actual hunt.

Small groups of hunters are spread out on either side of a limestone plateau above a broad, grassy valley. Below, there are several boggy areas, key elements in the hunters' strategy. The weather is cold and damp, and the men need the hides they wear draped over their shoulders for warmth. They have crouched on the frost-cracked ground all morning, waiting for the elephants to appear.

This is the fourth season the men have come, drawn by the expectation that the elephants will use this pass once again during their annual migration. The hunters are members of several bands that normally hunt and forage in separate areas during the rest of the year, but that join forces in autumn, when the oak leaves begin to turn yellow and the grass is dry. The men understand the importance of cooperation and work well together. Some are even related, sisters and daughters having been exchanged between bands. And thus around the fires at night there is an air of fraternity, enlivened, perhaps, by an acting out of the year's most exciting hunts.

The men are armed with fire-hardened wooden spears, bone daggers and stone weapons. These are not very impressive arms with which to take on such big prey, but the hunters also have another weapon at their disposal, and it is a weapon they know the elephants fear—fire. One man in each group is a fire-bearer, carrying a slow-burning torch, ready for use the moment the hunt begins.

When the men catch sight of the elephants moving slowly into the valley from the north, they hug the ground and wait for those out front—three bulls, two females and two juveniles—to come abreast of them. Then at a signal they rise and move down the slopes behind the animals. With the wind blowing toward the bogs, they set a long arc of fire in the sear grass and slowly move forward as the flames close in on the trapped animals. Suddenly the ground shakes under the hunters' feet as the elephants stampede away from the crackling fire toward the bog. Three adult animals and two juveniles sink into the deep, sticky mud, and the shouting men approach behind the fire to dispatch them.

As the hunters move closer, a few terrified wild horses, ensnared along with the larger beasts, charge out through the encircling flames in frantic flight. Several hunters leap upon the escaping prey, hanging on as they jab at the horses with spears and sharply pointed bones until the animals collapse on the smouldering valley floor.

Now the work of killing the mired elephants begins. The hunters, light enough to avoid being mired, duck the flailing trunks and attack. Some thrust spears at the beasts, others pummel the animals' heads with stones. The great beasts shriek in rage and pain as the men close in for the kill. As the last elephant rolls over into mud, the men fall upon them eagerly. Here, in these mountains of flesh and bone, is enough meat to feed their several bands all they could possibly eat.

Such a detailed reconstruction, though speculative, is based on the evidence uncovered at the site of the hunt. And how this evidence came to light is a fascinating story in its own right. The relics at Torralba and Ambrona, like those at Terra Amata, were first hit upon accidentally by a commercial enterprise. In 1888 workers for a Belgian company were digging trenches in preparation for laying a water main for a railroad when they came upon a few huge bones; these turned out to be the remains of an extinct species of huge elephant *(Elephas antiquus)*, which had straight, rather than curved, tusks almost 10 feet long. The bones remained only curiosities until 1907 when a Spanish aristocrat, the Marqués de Cerralbo, an amateur archeologist, began to excavate at Torralba. Off and on for four years the Marqués dug and collected

Stampeded by fires into a bog, an elephant is stabbed and stoned to death. For their wooden spears to penetrate an elephant's thick hide, the hunters hardened the points in their fires and then sharpened them with a denticulate (inset), a flaked stone tool with a serrated and notched edge.

fossils, including the remains of at least 25 elephants. He also found several kinds of stone and bone tools, sharpened tusks and fragments of wood, apparently worked by man—the first collection of Homo erectus artifacts ever assembled.

The Marqués himself was a considerable figure. A handsome man with a luxuriant blond mustache, he was one of Spain's grandest grandees, having inherited five other titles besides that of Cerralbo. He spent a lifetime collecting—a single peseta piece was the beginning of a boyhood coin collection that eventually numbered 22,000, the greatest in the world at the time—and his palace in Madrid, now the Cerralbo Museum, houses a rich trove of tapestries, paintings, porcelains and armor.

He was also his country's leading archeologist. At the time he started excavating Torralba, he had already led digs at 52 sites across the world, from Spain to the Orient. Torralba, a site that lay almost literally in his own backyard, was his crowning achievement, and he published a lengthy monograph on his findings there. In 1913 he became president of the Spanish Academy and spent his last decade as host to a procession of the world's leading scientists, artists and historians, who traveled to see his collections and evaluate the conclusions he had drawn from his archeological discoveries.

Cerralbo's work was justly celebrated, and many of his conclusions were sound—his conjecture that Torralba represented the most ancient site of a human settlement in Europe held good until discoveries at Vallonet in France in 1958—but his digging was hardly systematic by today's standards. A great deal of work still remained to be done at Torralba, but it was more than half a century before anyone did it.

Then in 1960 F. Clark Howell, University of Chicago anthropologist noted for his excavation of various prehistoric sites in Europe, Africa and the Middle East, visited the Marqués' old trenches and soil heaps. A quick examination told him that this was still rich ground, and the following year he came back to begin new excavations.

During one summer's work Howell and his assistants unearthed the remains of six additional elephants at Torralba and another dozen at Ambrona. By the end of the third season the diggers, under the direction of Howell's associate, anthropologist L. G. Freeman Jr., had found more than 50—with the promise of still others to come. Although Torralba was completely excavated, Howell had uncovered only a part of Ambrona before he turned his attention to the Omo River in Ethiopia, where Australopithecine remains had been found. (He noted that he was reserving the less strenuous job of excavating the rest of Ambrona for his old age.)

The unexplored portion of Ambrona may yet reveal the skeleton of Homo erectus. Neither the Marqués de Cerralbo nor Howell discovered any human fossils or evidence of man-made shelters at either site, but the picture of the hunting and butchering activities that emerged from the digs is the most complete we have for Homo erectus. It is even possible to tell what the climate and terrain were like at the time. The study of fossilized pollen has revealed that it was very cold in central Spain at some point during the period, so cold that the ground bore characteristic traces of frost-patterning, resembling land in northern Alaska today. The summers were only warm enough to have thawed out the surface; the subsurface remained frozen the year round. During the winter, when the top layer froze again, the water trapped between the two frozen layers expanded and, exerting tremendous pressure, began to ooze out, creating frost boils, muddy pockets in the ground. Elsewhere, the frost heaved the earth into mounds, and small rocks rolled down the sides to form rings of varying circumferences. (Such circles can look man-made and at least one student of prehistory thought they represented the remains of huts, such as were built at Terra Amata.)

Digging into this once-frozen soil, Howell found evidence that suggested to him that the hunters used fire to stampede the elephants: bits of charcoal and carbon widely scattered across the valley. The assumption that the men had spears as well as stone weapons is based on the discovery of small pieces of wood; one fragment, in rotting away, left a hollow in the ground that could be filled with plaster to reveal its original pointed shape.

The animal bones the hunters left behind reveal how the meat was butchered—and lead to intriguing speculations about Homo erectus' customs. After stripping the carcasses of choice pieces of flesh the hunters took the chunks of meat to a second spot nearby for further processing. Here, the debris they left behind would seem to indicate, they reduced it to smaller pieces and cracked some of the bones for marrow. What they did with the skulls is a mystery; only one was found, and it had a hole smashed in the top, presumably so the brain, a delicacy, could be extracted and eaten.

Once the hunters had cut up the meat, they seem to have feasted on it at other locations, marked by clusters of crushed and burned bones. But when the 20-ton size of an individual elephant is taken into account, it hardly seems possible that the hunters, no matter how numerous, could have eaten anything but a very small portion of the meat. They must have carried most of it off to their base camps, perhaps in some preserved form—possibly dried. Sir Samuel Baker, the 19th Century English explorer, reported seeing African hunters slice the flesh of elephants into long strips after a fire hunt, dry it and then smoke it on frames of green wood. The meat was then divided among the different villages that had assisted in the hunt. Drying, of course, reduces the weight of meat by a considerable amount, renders it more easily transportable and preserves it for future use. The American Indians used to dry buffalo they killed; the flesh of an entire cow, cut up and dehydrated, weighed only 45 pounds at the end of the process. The smoke curing process seems advanced, perhaps, for Homo erectus, but there is no reason why he could not have learned to dry his meat in the sun, as many people do today.

How did the hunters go about sharing the meat? The ashes, bones and tools of Torralba and Ambrona cannot answer the question directly. But one small clue emerged from the excavations. Analysis of the clusters of splintered and burned bones showed that each pile contained examples of most or all of the animal species known to have been killed and butchered at the site. Thus the hunters would seem to have distributed the spoils of the hunt equally among themselves; such egalitarianism is in fact the mark of hunter-gatherers today.

Some of the bones uncovered at Torralba and Ambrona raise puzzling questions about Homo erectus' habits. In the case of one animal, the skeletal remains of the left side only were found lying in a semiarticulated position, skin side up. Although the cranium and pelvis had been removed, the bones do not appear to have been cracked for the marrow, as had many other specimens. Could this particular elephant have been singled out for special treatment and its bones assembled in a symbolic way, perhaps as part of a ritual? A more prosaic explanation may be that the animal stumbled into a boggy area, became stuck in the mud, tried to free itself and then toppled onto its left side, completely worn out. It may have sunk so deeply into the muck that only its right side could be butchered. But then why was the remaining part eventually flipped over, as the position of the skeleton would seem to indicate?

Across the valley at Ambrona a tusk and five long bones were discovered lying in a straight line near other parts of the animal's skeleton. It was at first thought that these huge bones may have served as a bridge across a boggy area, but in fact this particular spot was not a swamp at the time. Perhaps the alignment had a ritualistic meaning; the ancient Iberians, like some modern hunting peoples, might well have had a deep respect for their giant prey. There is, however, no direct evidence of any ritualistic practice among these hunters, so this suggestion is mere conjecture. And besides, it is quite clear that the practical hunters were not so reverent that they avoided turning parts of their prey into tools. Among the many artifacts found at Torralba were some that had been made from animals' long bones and ribs, which had been fractured longitudinally down the middle. The pieces were then flaked by stones used like hammers to produce tools that may have functioned as picks, cleavers or hand axes.

The Homo erectus hunters paid at least 10 visits to

Butchering a dead elephant, a hunter chops off a leg with a 10-inch cleaver (inset), a stone that has been shaped to a point and further chipped around the edges until it is sharp enough to cut through the toughest muscle and sinew. After the flesh is carved away, this prehistoric butcher will smash the leg bone with the same tool to extract the marrow.

Torralba, but Howell and his associates have not been able to determine whether the same groups were involved in each visit or how much time elapsed between the first visit and last. Nor have they been able to pinpoint just when in time the hunters came. The charcoal was too old for radiocarbon dating, and the river deposits were not suitable for the potassium-argon method of dating, which can be used only on lava and volcanic ash. The botanical and geological evidence indicated, however, that the ancient hunters were active at least 300,000 years ago—and probably close to 400,000 years ago.

The importance of Torralba and Ambrona, providing one of the oldest known examples of cooperative hunting, lies in the proof they afford that Homo erectus was capable not only of successful team effort but also of the coordination of the diverse social activities that the techniques of butchering and processing prey involved, apparently including the equitable distribution of meat.

The evidence also shows that Erectus' brain was advanced enough that he could project into the future on the basis of past experience—in other words, he could plan. He could memorize details about the expanse over which he wandered and remember how to get back to camp. More significant, he could perceive and follow the seasonal migrations of the animals he hunted. Thus hunting was no longer a hit-or-miss proposition, a matter of getting whatever game was around. Man had learned to take the initiative and go where the hunting was good. The Spanish site is by no means the only proof of such carefully planned forays. Terra Amata in southern France also was a camp where wandering hunters

stopped briefly at a certain time each year because that is where the animals were.

The travel imposed on Erectus by his wandering prey must have had an enormous effect on his life. It forced him to cover new ground and exposed him to a variety of new experiences and sensations. All primates are curious and, doubtless, Erectus explored the diverse features of his enlarging world with interest. He must have had to solve new problems, such as how to transport food and water and fire as he moved from one hunting ground to the next; no direct evidence has been discovered so far to show he had receptacles of any sort, but it is inconceivable that he could have managed without them—at least crude skin bags made of animal hides or perhaps bowls made of wood, stone or even clay. (It would seem unlikely that Erectus carried many stone tools with him; the elephant bones sharpened for use as tools at Torralba and the chips around the toolmaker's "bench" at Terra Amata suggest that he manufactured most of his implements on the spot.)

The hunters' wanderings may have played a part in Erectus' remarkable expansionary movement out of the tropics, if only in preparing him for the adjustments that the new environment would force on him. When he did begin to move from the tropics, the cooler climates he found made his taming of fire a necessity and also required clothing of some sort. This clothing was undoubtedly made from the pelts

To skin a young deer, two men work with deft strokes of a sidescraper (inset), a three-inch, double-edged tool of flint quickly made by striking a flake from a larger stone and sharpening the flake's edges. By starting at the belly and cutting toward head and tail and then down the inside of the deer's legs, the men can remove the hide in one piece.

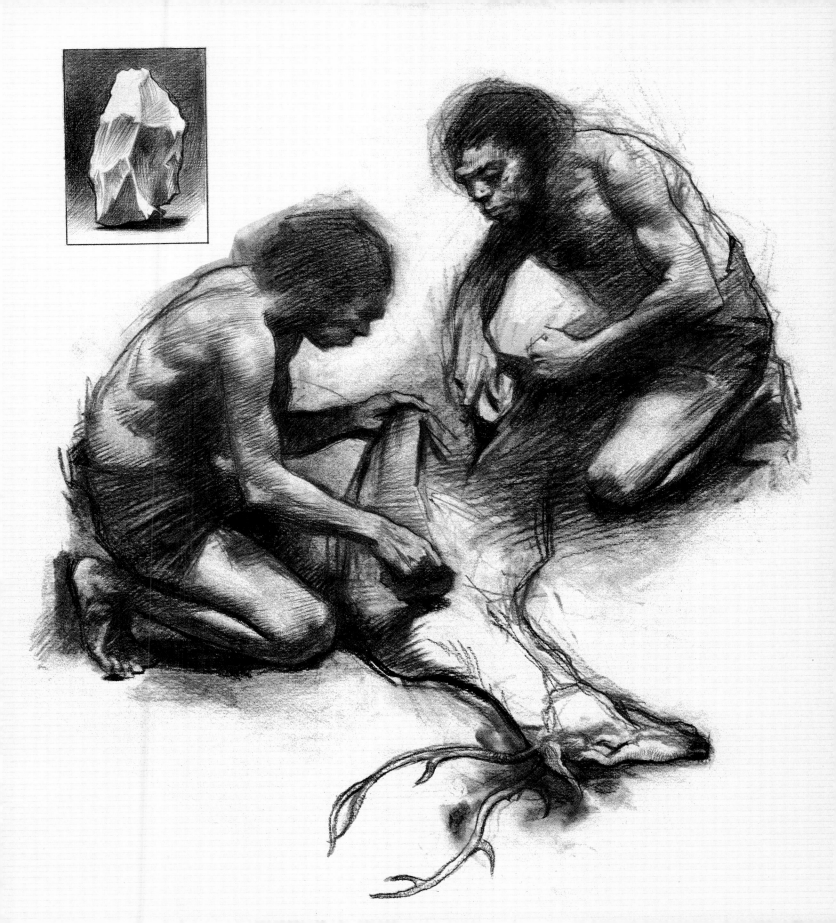

of the animals he killed—a revealing impression in the ground at Terra Amata shows he used hides for something. Cold, harsh winters also deprived him of the tropics' year-round supply of berries, fruits and vegetables, placing an even higher premium on his skill as a hunter.

How successfully he met these challenges is evident not only in southern France and Spain, but also almost 7,000 miles to the east in China at Choukoutien, near modern Peking (at very nearly the same latitude as Torralba). Here in hillside caves is evidence of man the hunter as he lived for perhaps 300,000 years. The floor of the excavated caves was a 130-foot-thick collection of refuse, laid down layer by layer, which contained the remains of leopards, saber-toothed tigers, huge hyenas, rhinoceroses and water buffalo, among other animals. The cave dwellers' favorite quarry, evidently, was deer: of all the animal bones found in the cave, some 70 per cent were deer remains. Some of these were taken there by oth-

er predators who from time to time moved into the caves when Peking man was not in residence—or could not evict his unwanted tenant—but the presence of burned bones and the contiguous layers of ash signify clearly that for many years men sat at their hearths and cooked and ate the venison they had stalked and killed.

The record of achievement left by Homo erectus at Choukoutien, Torralba-Ambrona, Terra Amata and other sites may not seem like much for his million-year tenure. And yet in successfully adopting hunting as a way of life he had taken a major step toward establishing the genus Homo as supreme among the creatures of the earth. That style of life, though it would be modified and embellished and refined in the eons to come, set the pattern by which his Homo sapiens descendants would live almost to the dawn of historic times, when the invention of farming once again revolutionized the way in which a man supported himself and his family.

Unearthing a Scene of an Ancient Feast

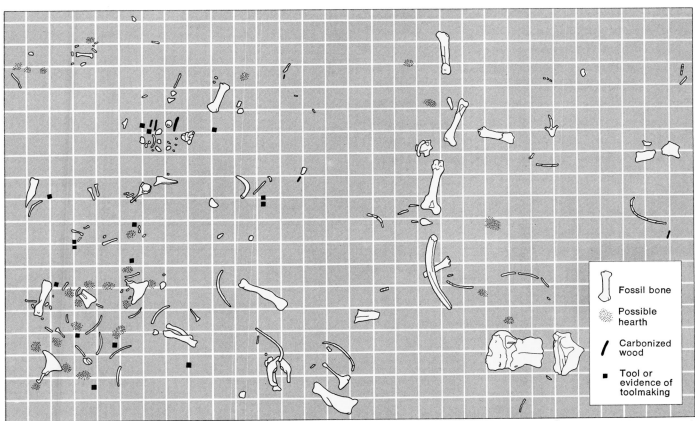

Fossil bone

Possible hearth

Carbonized wood

Tool or evidence of toolmaking

A blueprint of a prehistoric site, this plan is keyed to identify finds made at one section of a dig at Ambrona, Spain (pages 94-95).

Almost half a million years ago, near what is now the village of Ambrona, Spain, Homo erectus hunters cut up their kill and feasted, leaving behind a litter of fossil bones, tools and stones to intrigue present-day diggers. The diagram above, representing a part of the butchering and banqueting site, might seem to be no more than a prehistoric garbage dump. But thanks to the systematic techniques used by the excavator, anthropologist F. Clark Howell, this chaotic jumble actually discloses a wealth of information about the habits of Homo erectus.

To locate the long-hidden level where the bones and other artifacts had been left, Howell first sank a narrow trench into the hillside. Only when he got down to the level where remains appeared did he begin to dig more widely, carefully plotting the position of every object discovered. The picture that finally emerged reveals that a score or more of these early hunters had cooperated in killing elephants, a rhinoceros, some deer, a monkey and some birds. On the following pages the steps in uncovering one section of the Ambrona site are depicted in models, prepared under Howell's guidance, that show how the past can be exposed layer by layer.

First Step: Slicing a Trench into a Hillside

Looking for a sign of ancient human activity at the Ambrona site, the diggers sank an exploratory slit trench into the hillside. In the model, the man in the foreground has already uncovered a fossil elephant skull, and pick and shovel men on the steps above him are starting to clear away overlying deposits, preliminary to the more exacting task of digging out a broad section of the site.

Unknown to Howell, Ambrona was first tested in the early 1900s by the Marqués de Cerralbo, a Spanish archeologist who had found Homo erectus cultural remains at nearby Torralba, a mile away. A half-century later, when Howell was excavating at Torralba, he asked the local people if they knew of any similar places with bones like these. One farmer from Ambrona village replied, "Yes, on the land I cultivate in Ambrona."

Howell got the man's permission to dig a test trench on his land. The first excavation turned up some fossils, and additional exploration laid the groundwork for a dig that was to spread over several plots of farmland. Excavation equipment was brought in from Madrid and shortly the Ambrona site was revealing its ancient past.

Loosened soil is removed from the various trench levels in baskets and wheelbarrows, to be carefully

sifted for any traces of *Homo erectus*. The sign to the right of the man overseeing the work warns off anyone who is not directly involved in the dig.

Wider Excavation of the Trench for a Full-Scale Dig

Even before the first telltale elephant skull was fully uncovered, the diggers at Ambrona started to expand the slit trench horizontally to expose a larger area of the site. The model shows how layer after layer of earth deposits are stripped off to open up a site, while an assistant *(left)* makes drawings and notes that eventually produce a detailed ground plan like the one on page 87. Other assistants, shown to the right of the excavation in the model, prepare the way for further exploration. One of them, kneeling near the "No trespassing" sign, measures off the ground into three-meter squares and hammers down metal corner stakes forged by the local blacksmith. His companion ties string to the stakes to mark off the digging surface clearly. Each square is numbered and everything dug up within it is tagged with that number and is noted on a grid to indicate the level at which it was uncovered. With such meticulous identification, each find can later be precisely located on a master sketch of its level—and in this way the activities of a particular time period can be related. For example, stone tools and animal bones, dug out from the same layer but adjoining trenches, are linked to the same time and place —perhaps indicating the tools were used to cut up the animal.

The level first uncovered is reddish silt, laid down by floods hundreds of thousands of years ago.

Underlying it is a gray deposit. In the marl just above the animal remains, plant pollen indicated the vegetation and climate existing at the time.

The Delicate Task of Freeing Long-buried Relics

When the rough pick and shovel work was finished and the long-concealed traces of Homo erectus' sojourn at Ambrona began to appear through the last few inches of soil, the most demanding work still remained to be done. The model shows assistants deftly loosening the hard-packed soil from around bones and artifacts and carefully whisking it away with fine brushes. The excess soil, swept into piles with brooms, was scooped up in short-handled shovels and carted elsewhere in wheelbarrows to be sifted through fine-mesh screens. All finds were left in place until the assistant in the right foreground recorded them and their relation to one another on his excavation plan. Then they were removed from the ground. When bone was found that was too fragile to be taken away for study, it was usually strengthened with a hardening agent or jacketed in plaster.

Even before the site was completely exposed, the diggers were confronted with some puzzling relics of early man. To the right in the model are a pair of elephant thigh bones and a tusk—all strangely lined up. At bottom right another enigma can be seen: an almost complete elephant skull. All the other skulls found at Ambrona and Torralba had been shattered so that the brains could be removed and eaten; why this skull should have survived with only the top missing is a tantalizing mystery.

At the level of the ancient campsite archeologists cautiously uncover the earth around the remains of

Erectus' feast. Their work is still guided by the three-meter-square grids (indicated by the stakes), which were lowered as the digging progressed.

The Remains of an Erectus Hunt Brought to Light

Except for a broom and a metric surveyor's rod, the fully exposed portion of the site re-created in this model looks much as Homo erectus left it one day over 300 millennia ago. The bones to the right include the aligned tusk and bones from the left side of an elephant. Other elephant bones toward the center foreground include a complete lower jaw, parts of a forelimb and several ribs and vertebrae. The concentrations of small stones at the left present an enigma to anthropologists, who are certain from the stones' composition that they could neither have been there naturally nor have been washed down by ancient streams. Erectus brought them, but his purpose in doing so is unclear, and Howell for one refuses to speculate about their use. Perhaps they were used as hearths, since fractured and broken bones of wild oxen, horses, deer and elephants strewn around them indicate the area may have been a cooking and eating site. Scattered throughout the area and indicated in blue are a number of stone tools and many pieces of stone left over from toolmaking.

All that is lacking in this model of butchering and feasting is Erectus himself. Despite all the other evidence that Erectus camped here—such as the stone tools and the remnants of fire, which he was the first to use —Howell's digging at Ambrona yielded not a single human bone or tooth.

Missing only the bloodstains from the butchering, the bits of flesh and the grease spots that must

have marked the soil after a hearty meal, the completely exposed campsite mutely testifies to the success of the hunting skills of Homo erectus.

When did man learn to speak? How did he start? What did his first words sound like? Investigators have been seeking answers to questions like these for thousands of years. In ancient Egypt the pharaoh Psammetichus ordered two infants reared where they could hear no human voices. He hoped that when at last they spoke, uninfluenced by the sound of the Egyptian tongue, they would resort to their earliest ancestors' language, which he confidently presumed lurked within them. One child finally uttered something that sounded like *bekos,* or "bread," in the language of Phrygia, an ancient nation of central Asia Minor. Ergo, said Psammetichus triumphantly, Phrygian was obviously man's original tongue.

Many centuries later King James IV of Scotland tried a similar experiment with two bairns. The result, he let it be known, was that his human guinea pigs spoke passable Hebrew. This report must have pleased Biblical scholars of the day, for they had contended all along that Adam and Eve conversed in Hebrew. A chauvinistic Swede of the late 17th Century believed otherwise: he announced that in the Garden of Eden God used Swedish, Adam Danish and the serpent French.

As time went on, all sorts of theories sprang up concerning the origins of speech. The 18th Century French philosopher Rousseau envisioned a group of tongue-tied men getting together and stammering out more or less overnight a language they could use.

Speech is made visible for analysis by a sound spectrograph, which electronically translates sounds into loudness and pitch diagrams on a drum (far left). Linguists extrapolate from sound pictures of humans and nonhuman primates, and also compare the vocal apparatus of early and modern men, to tell how the speech of Homo erectus might have sounded (pages 106-107).

Why they felt the need for one, and how they communicated with each other before they had invented the words to communicate with, Rousseau failed to mention. His contemporary, the German romanticist Johann Gottfried Herder, also espoused the notion that language was man-made, not God-instilled as most people believed. Anything so illogical, so imperfect as language could hardly be attributed to a divinity, he argued. But he would have none of Rousseau's simple-mindedness either. Instead, he saw language springing from the innermost nature of man, in response to an impulse to speak. Just how language took shape Herder could not say, but he imagined that it started when man began imitating sounds of the creatures around him—and that the imitations became the words for the animals themselves. This theory, known today among its detractors as the bow-wow thesis, was followed by a spate of others, similarly named and ridiculed, including the whistle and grunt thesis, the ding-dong, the ee-ee and even the ouch-ouch, which claimed that language rose from ejaculations of pain, pleasure, fear, surprise, and so on.

Scientists still do not know the full story of the origin of language, but—thanks to Darwin and the concept of human evolution, which provided a new way of approaching the problem—they do have a fairly good idea of how man came to speak. Furthermore, they have good reason to believe that Homo erectus was the first creature to depend on language for communication. Studies of animals, particularly monkeys and apes, both in the laboratory and in the wild have given an understanding of the foundation on which language is based—and have shown that there is considerably more of the ape in talkative man than most people ever stop to think about. An examination of that foundation is necessary because understanding what communication was like before there were words helps make clear why and how language evolved, and emphasizes the tremendous changes that it made possible.

There are some intriguing ways of communicating among the lower animals and insects. Honeybees, for instance, perform a kind of dance on the honeycomb that accurately transmits information about the direction, distance and nature of a food source. Dogs and wolves employ scents to communicate, in addition to their barks, howls and growls, and they also use a system of visual signals that includes not only facial expression and body movement but also the position of the tail.

Communications get more complex as the social organizations of animals do, and next to ourselves the nonhuman primates have the most intricate systems of all. Far from depending primarily on vocalizations, as we might expect, the nonhuman primates seem to rely heavily on combinations of gestures, facial expressions and postures as well as sounds. They apparently are able to lend many shades of meaning to this body-language vocabulary, often using the sounds as a means of calling attention to their other signals. However, there are important occasions when only sounds will do. Discovering something good to eat, for example, a monkey or ape will let out a cry of pleasure that brings the rest of the troop running; or, sensing danger, it will give a shriek that causes its companions frantically to seek shelter.

This wordless communication system serves the nonhuman primates extremely well. As social animals living in troops, they use it to keep in touch with one another at all times. More important, it enables individuals to display their feelings, and to recognize at a glance the intentions of others, thus averting conflict. Many of the signals used have to do with dominance and submission, reinforcing the established hierarchy within the troop and making sure that every member knows his place. A subordinate male baboon, for example, seeing signs of aggression directed at him by a male of superior rank, backs up to the other and "presents" his rump in a gesture of appeasement—unless he intends to challenge the other male. Different signals, vocal and visual, keep the troop from becoming scattered when it is on the move or roaming over a territory foraging for food. Still other signals promote mating behavior and foster good mother-infant relations. A mother chimpanzee has been observed to calm her disturbed youngster simply by touching its finger lightly with hers. "So complex and so delicate is this language of gesture in the chimpanzee," says the physical anthropologist Bernard Campbell, "that it cannot be said to be less evolved than our own."

Yet for all its complexity, and however suited it may be to the chimpanzees' needs, such a communication system falls far short of human language. For one thing, it apparently expresses only emotion. As far as is known, nonhuman primates in the wild have no way of referring to their environment—they cannot name specific things—they cannot communicate thought via the complex phonetic codes men use. Nor do they seem able to refer to the past or future with the aid of their signals. For them, what is out of sight is out of mind.

This is not to say that the nonhuman primates' vocal signals are entirely unspecific. Some apes, for instance, indicate the desirability of the food they are eating by the intensity of their food calls. During normal feeding, chimpanzees emit food grunts, whereas bananas, a favorite food, elicit the more excited food bark. They still cannot say "banana," of course, but they have communicated something more than simply "food." Even more specialized is the danger call system of the African vervet monkeys, which have three different alarm calls for three different kinds of attackers. The vervets use a chutter for snakes, a chirp for ground-dwelling carnivores, and a "r-raup" sound to warn of birds of prey. A chirp is enough to send the vervets scrambling to the tips of branches, well out of reach of ground animals, while a "r-raup" launches them from the trees into the thickets below, where birds cannot get at them. A cry of "Watch out—eagle!" is beyond their capabilities, but it is also beyond their needs. They do not have to know whether it is an eagle or a hawk diving on them; what matters is that they get the message and flee in the right direction.

Humans, too, have a repertory of wordless signals that express emotions. A man has only to smile to demonstrate his friendly intentions; clenched fists and jaws, scowls and frowns are unmistakable signs of anger or disappointment throughout the world; the kiss, for all its complex social and erotic applications, is first of all a natural expression of affection. (These basic signals are in a different category from the many other body motions humans use, such as shaking and nodding the head, shrugging the shoulders, clapping the hands, which are really only abbreviated substitutes for spoken language and vary in meaning from one place to another.) Humans have even acquired at least one involuntary signal the oth-

er primates do not have, the blush, over which most people have little or no control, but which sends a clear message about what is going on inside the brain. And when humans are most excited, they often show it by speechlessness.

But these nonvocal signals are much less important to man than they are to other animals, for they make up a much smaller part of his communication system. Most of the vital information necessary for social interaction among men is conveyed vocally—a nonhuman primate would be almost helpless without its eyes, whereas a blind man is quite able to communicate. Speech, many authorities believe, is what makes humans human, a belief supported by the tragedy of a baby born deaf. He is almost an exile from his race. Since he cannot hear and imitate spoken words, it is very difficult to teach him to speak—and without speech he is reduced to communicating clumsily and inadequately.

The gift of language provides a magnificently efficient and versatile system of communication. Its coded series of sounds conveys thought at least 10 times faster than any other method of signaling possibly can—faster than hand signs, moving pictures or even other kinds of vocalization. Language is man's passport to a totally new level of social organization, the tool that allows him to vary his behavior to meet changing conditions instead of being limited by less flexible action patterns, as the other primates are. Through language man can step outside himself and give things names, reflect about them and refer to them in the past and the future. Most important of all, language gives man the capacity to share his thoughts. As Sherwood L. Washburn and Shirley C. Strum have written in a paper on hu-

Silent Signals That Aid Talking

Communication without words —based primarily on signs like those used by primitive tribesmen today—may have supplemented the speech of Homo erectus, whose language could not have been as complex and fluent as that of modern man. In a society where the structure of life is relatively simple, as it was in the time of Homo erectus, signs alone can convey a remarkable amount of essential information.

The Sibiller tribesmen of present-day New Guinea, for example, form numbers by counting on their fingers and other parts of the body (*top row at right*). A Bushman hunter of South Africa, necessarily silent as he stalks an animal, relies on sign language to identify the prey for fellow hunters; in the two lower rows of pictures, he uses his fingers and arm to mimic the animal's most characteristic feature— describing it as effectively as any spoken word.

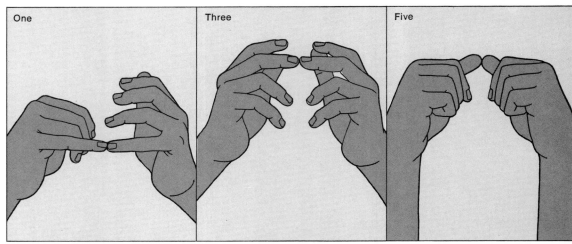

By matching the fingers of both hands, then pointing to parts of his left arm and his ear, eye and nose, o

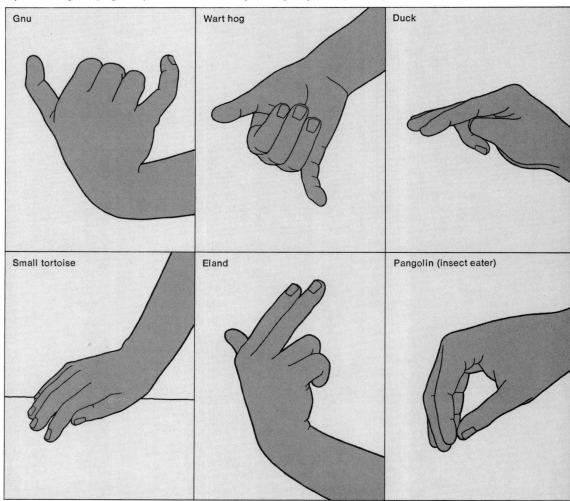

Bushmen keep their hunting companions informed by hand signals suggesting each animal's hallmark, such

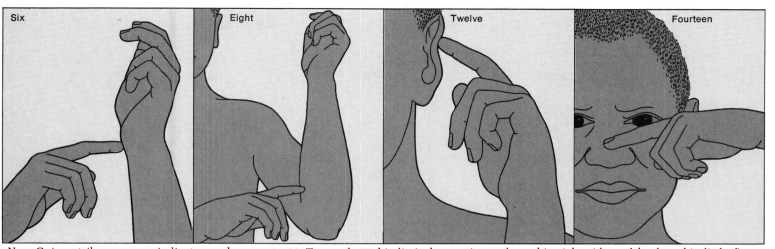

New Guinea tribesman can indicate numbers up to 14. To reach 27, his limit, he continues down his right side and back to his little fingers.

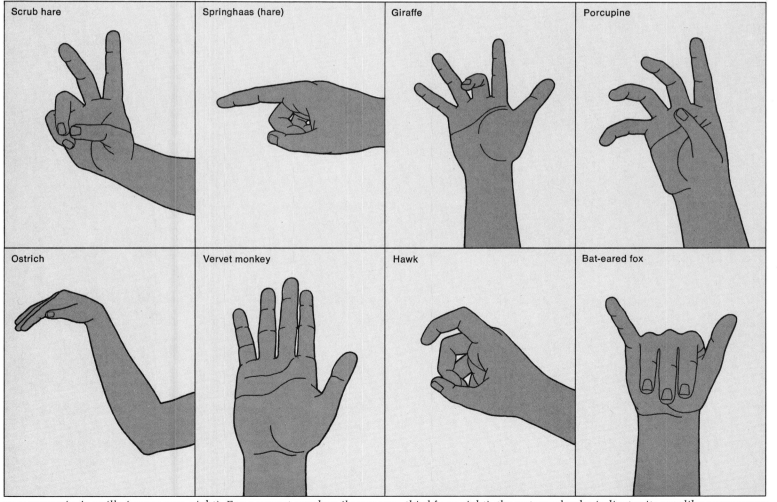

as a porcupine's quills (upper row, right). For a vervet monkey (lower row, third from right), the upturned palm indicates its manlike appearance.

man evolution: "It is the communication of thought, rather than thought itself, that is unique to man, makes human cultures possible, and that is the primary factor in separating man and beast."

This insight provides one of the reasons why specialists are so sure Homo erectus must have had some form of language: so many of the activities he engaged in required a sharing of thought. To execute a hunt such as that documented in the fossil evidence at Torralba-Ambrona, for instance, he must have been able to lay plans in advance, name animals, plants and tools, identify places and refer to both the past and future. Moreover, the division of labor that marked Homo erectus society would have been all but impossible if men and women had been unable to communicate about their separate responsibilities, or could not agree to meet at a particular spot once their food-gathering activities were over. As their society grew more complex, they would have used words to sort out family relationships and to establish ties with neighboring bands.

Furthermore, language was the new means by which man acquired and passed on from one generation to the next that flexible network of learned, rather than inherited, behavior patterns that allowed him to alter his environment and adapt to new ones. This was the beginning of culture. From this point in the evolution of man, culture and its medium, language, would be necessary for survival.

Though it has long been clear that this watershed in evolution occurred largely because of the ability to use words to communicate symbolic meaning, it was not at all clear until recently why man alone, and not his close, intelligent relatives among the apes, learned to speak. After all, apes have much of the vocal apparatus—lips, a tongue and a larynx, or voice box with vocal cords—that men do. Yet they cannot learn to talk as humans do, as repeated experiments have shown. One of the first men to toy with the idea was an 18th Century French physician and philosopher, Julien Offray de Lamettrie, who imagined that apes were on about the same intellectual level as retarded humans and that all they needed to turn them into "perfect little gentlemen" was speech training. Not until the early 20th Century, however, were any scientific attempts made to teach apes to talk. One couple worked with a chimpanzee called Viki, and only after six years of the most painstaking effort on their part—and a great deal of frustration on hers—did she manage to say, on cue, what sounded like "Mama," "Papa," "up" and "cup."

A more recent experiment produced a more startling result. A chimp named Washoe was taught to understand, by the age of five, more than 350 hand signals of a standard sign language of the deaf and to use at least 150 of them correctly. With these, she learned to name things and express her wants and needs in terms of those names. Naming things is of course a kind of symbolization, and in that limited sense Washoe learned to communicate like a human. But sign language is not speech.

Washoe's success and Viki's frustration have led to a clearer understanding of what is involved in human speech. There is some equipment, both physical and mental, necessary for spoken language, that apes and monkeys simply do not have. The adult human tongue, for example, is thicker than that of the monkeys and apes and, unlike theirs, it bends in a sharp right angle into the throat. In addition, the human larynx lies farther down in the throat than the

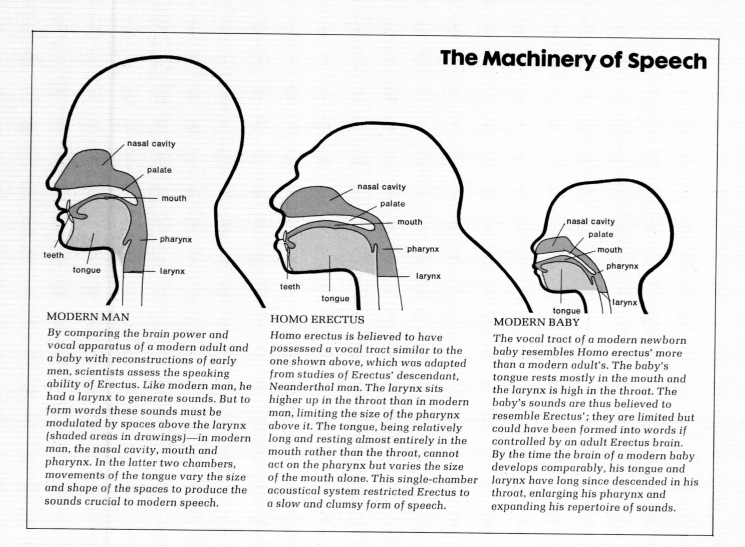

The Machinery of Speech

MODERN MAN

By comparing the brain power and vocal apparatus of a modern adult and a baby with reconstructions of early men, scientists assess the speaking ability of Erectus. Like modern man, he had a larynx to generate sounds. But to form words these sounds must be modulated by spaces above the larynx (shaded areas in drawings)—in modern man, the nasal cavity, mouth and pharynx. In the latter two chambers, movements of the tongue vary the size and shape of the spaces to produce the sounds crucial to modern speech.

HOMO ERECTUS

Homo erectus is believed to have possessed a vocal tract similar to the one shown above, which was adapted from studies of Erectus' descendant, Neanderthal man. The larynx sits higher up in the throat than in modern man, limiting the size of the pharynx above it. The tongue, being relatively long and resting almost entirely in the mouth rather than the throat, cannot act on the pharynx but varies the size of the mouth alone. This single-chamber acoustical system restricted Erectus to a slow and clumsy form of speech.

MODERN BABY

The vocal tract of a modern newborn baby resembles Homo erectus' more than a modern adult's. The baby's tongue rests mostly in the mouth and the larynx is high in the throat. The baby's sounds are thus believed to resemble Erectus'; they are limited but could have been formed into words if controlled by an adult Erectus brain. By the time the brain of a modern baby develops comparably, his tongue and larynx have long since descended in his throat, enlarging his pharynx and expanding his repertoire of sounds.

ape larynx. This means that the part of the throat above the larynx, the pharynx, is proportionately much larger in humans than in any other primates.

The pharynx serves as a combined opening for the windpipe, which goes to the lungs, and the gullet, leading to the stomach; but it is also the anchor for the base of the tongue, and it plays a fundamental part in the production of speech. For it is the pharynx that plays a major role in modifying the sounds made by the vocal cords and in giving them the shape that a listener recognizes as language. To provide this control, the muscles of the pharynx walls and the base of the tongue move continually during speech, constantly and precisely varying the dimensions of the pharynx—its greatest width is at least 10 times its narrowest. These dimensional changes produce

much the same effect on sounds that an organ achieves with its dozens of pipes of different lengths and diameters, each making a particular tone. So important is the pharynx to speech that it is quite possible to speak intelligibly without the larynx or tip of the tongue—that part we show when the doctor asks us to say "aaah"—as long as the pharynx and base of the tongue are intact.

Monkeys and apes, lacking the mental and vocal equipment of man, vary the shape of only their mouths when they vocalize, and there is practically no movement of the pharynx, which is in any case quite rudimentary; they can produce only a certain number of distinct signal sounds—10 to 15 in most cases—and they cannot combine them at will to form words. (The greatest number of different sounds that can be made by any species of monkey or ape is the 25 vocalizations of the Japanese macaque.)

The same limitation, in fact, restricts the vocalization of human babies, who at birth are unable to make the vowel sounds typical of modern human speech. For at least six weeks a baby's tongue remains immobile during his cries. Moreover, his tongue rests almost entirely within the mouth, as in nonhuman primates, and the larynx sits high in his throat. This arrangement permits the baby to swallow and breathe at the same time without danger of choking. By the time he reaches the babbling stage, at around three months, the base of the tongue and the larynx have already begun to descend into the throat, enlarging the pharyngeal region—and not until then is the infant equipped physically to make the speech sounds that will distinguish him from his simian ancestors.

There are other equally important reasons why men can talk and the nonhuman primates cannot; they have to do with the brain. When a man uses his voice to communicate, he does more, of course, than make noise. He is in fact codifying thought and transmitting it to others in a string of connected sounds. The coding begins in the cerebral cortex, the convoluted outer layer of the brain. Here lie three areas of particular importance in speech production. One is called Broca's area. Located toward the front of the dominant hemisphere, it sends the code to an adjacent part of the brain controlling muscles of the face, jaw, tongue, palate and larynx and thus helps set the speech apparatus in operation. Injury to Broca's area produces one form of aphasia—loss or impairment of speech—in which articulation is slow and labored.

The Controls of Speech

Man's ability to speak depends as much on the structure of his brain as it does on his vocal apparatus (page 103). Homo erectus' vocal tract is believed to be more like a modern newborn baby's than an adult's, which means that he probably talked slowly and clumsily. But his brain must already have had the beginnings of modern man's three primary language areas (top drawing), which are located on the surface of one side of the outer, thinking layer of the brain.

One area, the angular gyrus, is a linking station that integrates signals from man's senses of sight, hearing and touch to prompt a verbal response. It works with Wernicke's area, which serves as a language selector, retrieving from the brain's filing cabinet the words appropriate to the interpretations of the angular gyrus. The mechanics of talking are operated by Broca's area, which transmits signals for words to adjacent nerve centers controlling muscles of the face, lips, tongue and larynx. Connecting Broca's area and Wernicke's area and sweeping by the angular gyrus is the arcuate fasciculus (center drawing), a pathway of nerve fibers beneath the speech centers.

Nonverbal communications—cries of pain or pleasure, or gestures—are controlled by the limbic system (bottom drawing) deep in the center of the brain. Homo erectus, his speech abilities still rather limited, probably used this center of communication more than modern man does.

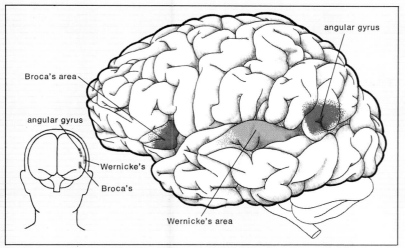

Brain speech areas, shown above, are on the surface on one side (inset).

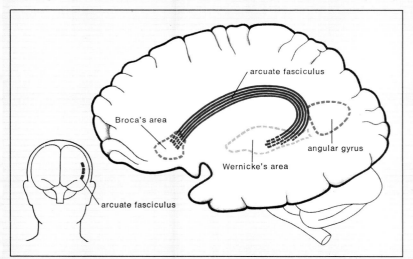

A subsurface nerve bundle loops to connect Broca's and Wernicke's areas.

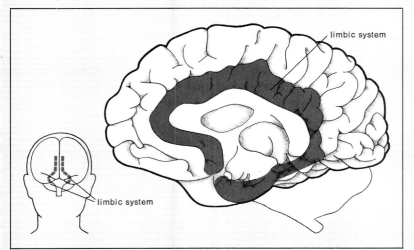

The limbic system for nonverbal communication is in both brain halves.

The second region is Wernicke's area, located farther back in the brain, in the temporal lobe, and vital to the process of comprehension; thus damage to Wernicke's area usually produces another form of aphasia: speech that is fluent but meaningless. An almost unpronounceable bundle of nerve fibers, called the arcuate fasciculus, apparently transmits auditory patterns from Wernicke's area to Broca's, making possible the vocal repetition of a heard word.

The third region, adjacent to Wernicke's area, is known as the angular gyrus, and it occupies a key position at the juncture of individual portions of the cerebral cortex that are concerned with vision, hearing and touch—the parts of the brain that receive information from the world outside the body. Linked to these sensory receivers by bundles of nerve fibers, the angular gyrus operates as a kind of connecting station, permitting one type of incoming signal to be associated with others. For example, the angular gyrus makes it possible for the brain to link the visual stimulus produced by the sight of a cup with the aural stimulus produced by a voice saying "cup" and with the tactile stimulus produced when the hand picks up the cup. The importance of these associations as far as speech is concerned is clear when we think of the way children learn the words for things: when a child asks, "What's that?" and is told by his parents, he matches the image of the seen object with the sound of the spoken word—and thus absorbs the name for it, automatically filing the auditory code for that association in his memory bank. This process of association and memorization is the first and most basic step in the acquisition of language.

The brains of monkeys and apes are similar to humans', but significantly less developed in some

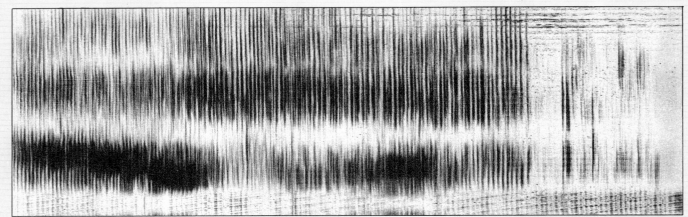

A sound spectrogram, or visual picture, of the "aaah" cry of a newborn baby shows its tones (dark areas) to be quite limited.

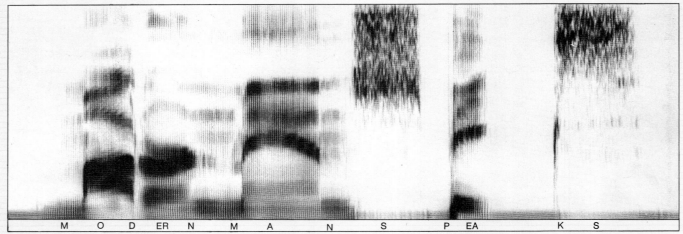

M   O   D   ER   N   M   A   N   S   P   EA   K   S

Many discrete tones over a wide range create the vowels and consonants that enable an adult to say "modern man speaks."

important areas. The angular gyrus is so small that there can be practically no association between information signals coming from the senses. Apparently incoming signals are routed mainly to another part of the brain altogether—the limbic system. All vertebrate animals, including man, have this evolutionarily ancient subregion lying at the core of the brain, a kind of netherworld of neurological activity. Among other things, it activates the physical responses that go with hunger, fear, rage and sexual activity. It also triggers the feelings that accompany these responses. So that if a monkey sees an enemy, for instance, the visual signal feeds into the limbic system and produces a physical reaction—the sounding

of the danger call, perhaps—and also makes the animal feel fear. Similarly, sexual signals sent out by a female chimpanzee go to the limbic system of a male, causing him to feel sexually stimulated and prompting a suitable response.

In other words, information channeled to the limbic system from the outside produces an instantaneous, unthinking response—or, as Rutgers University anthropologist Jane Lancaster has written, the limbic system "makes the animal want to do what it has to do to survive and reproduce."

Among the responses directed by the limbic system are vocal signals—cries of fear or pleasure, for example. That such communication is controlled by

The Sounds
of Speech

The wavering bands and squiggles in the pictures at left are what human voices look like when given visible form by a device called a sound spectrograph (page 96). Although such pictures are used primarily to analyze the speech of modern man, it is possible to deduce from them how well early man could talk.

By charting loudness (the relative darkness of the lines) and pitch (the vertical position of the dark bands), the diagrams can indicate which vowel and consonant sounds are present in vocalizations. A newborn baby's voice (top) consists mainly of the cry "aaah," made up of two almost unvarying components. It cannot generate some of the isolated, modulated components needed to create such vowels as the "a" or "eeeh" produced by an adult saying "modern man speaks" (bottom). Homo erectus, like the baby, lacked the anatomical mechanism of the vocal tract (page 103) needed to make the more complicated sounds of the modern adult. But the brain of an adult Homo erectus was probably sufficiently well developed for him to have established a language of his own based on the speech signals at his command.

this part of the brain can be demonstrated by laboratory experiment. When electrodes are planted in the limbic system and related structures of a monkey, and its brain is stimulated electrically, the animal responds with its repertory of cries, even though none of the situations that normally stimulate those sounds—aggressive behavior by a dominant male, food, enemies—is visible. Furthermore, other monkeys of the same species in the laboratory react to these sounds—by cringing, searching for food, taking an alert stance—just as though they were bona fide signals.

Similar experiments have been performed on human subjects during brain surgery, and they react in a similar way. When the human limbic system is stimulated, the patient also responds with sounds—a deep, primal cry, as it were. But these sounds produced through the limbic system in both ape and man are not the sounds of speech. For that distinctive emblem of humanness it was necessary for other parts of the brain—the angular gyrus, Broca's and Wernicke's areas—to develop fully, and it was in this development that emerging man left the inarticulate apes far behind.

It is impossible to pinpoint the time when Homo erectus began to use language. His period on earth spanned one million years and of course he was evolving all that time—the development of speech and other human characteristics was infinitely gradual. The process must have begun long before the first man, when his ancestors started making and using tools. If before then these proto-men had depended upon gestures to communicate, such hand signals would now have become inadequate—the hominids would literally have had their hands full, carrying tools to chop, cut or scrape. Thus the ability to use sounds to make meaning clear would have proved a great advantage.

But in order for the process of naming things to start, the vocal apparatus had to be modified, the brain rewired. This development must have taken hundreds of thousands of years during the evolution of man's immediate predecessor, Australopithecus. Some small mutations may have enabled the advanced Australopithecines to make a few more sounds than the other primates, giving them an edge in the competition for survival. The ability to signal one another through a more extensive call system would have been a definite advantage when they were gathering food or hunting. And then, as the number of vocalizations grew, brain development could have permitted more precise differentiation between calls, and primitive words may have taken shape. All the while the brain and vocal apparatus would have been involved in a feedback relationship with each other, changes in one fostering development of the other: the brain's success in forming a rudimentary sound code would have affected the vocal apparatus, and this, in turn, would have helped enlarge the speech centers of the brain, and so on until, by the time of Homo erectus, the rudiments of language would have appeared. At that point, the first men were ready to begin combining a few separate sounds, or words, that represented specific elements of terrain, the hunt, the family and seasonal changes into simple combinations that nevertheless conveyed a great deal of information.

What this first human speech sounded like depended on how far the dual development of vocal apparatus and brain equipment had progressed in Homo erectus. Recent investigations have given a glimmering of the state of that development. Philip Lieberman, a linguist at the University of Connecticut, has made an analysis of the character of modern speech that emphasizes the importance of man's vocal equipment. He points out that the pharynx is essential for producing the vowel sounds *a* ("ah"), *i* ("ee") and *u* ("oo"), which are crucial to all modern language, whether it is English or Kirghiz. Virtually all meaningful segments of human speech contain one or more of these sounds; combining them with a wide assortment of consonants, the human vocal apparatus not only can produce an infinite number of

variations but also—and more importantly—it can connect them with great rapidity in the coded series of sounds that is language.

The key to this process is the putting together of separate phonetic segments into a sound that is understood as one word. When a man says the word "bat," for instance, he does not articulate the fragments of sound represented by the letters b-a-t; rather he combines these elements into a single syllable. In this way the voice has the ability to put together and meaningfully transmit upward of 30 phonetic segments a second.

Had the pharynx developed enough in Homo erectus to produce such sounds, the complex ones characteristic of modern man? Lieberman thinks not. He places Erectus' speech at a much cruder level, basing this opinion on a fascinating piece of detective work carried out with the aid of Dr. Edmund S. Crelin, an anatomist at Yale's medical school. Much of this work involved fossils and reconstructions of Homo erectus' descendant, the type of Homo sapiens called Neanderthal man, but Lieberman feels the conclusions can be used to assess the development of Erectus as well. The two scientists compared the skulls of newborn modern babies, modern apes and Neanderthal man; they found many likenesses—indeed, in some ways, the skulls of modern babies were more similar to those of apes and early man than they were to that of a modern adult.

To get precisely detailed information about the all-important pharyngeal region located at the base of the skull, Crelin reconstructed the vocal tracts of several fossil men. Taking into account the anatomical similarities between the skull of Neanderthal man and those of modern apes and human infants, Crelin was able to estimate the position of the larynx in the throats of his fossil men—it was placed much higher than it is now. He then proceeded to reconstruct early man's pharyngeal, nasal and oral cavities in modeling clay. Then Lieberman measured the reconstructed vocal tracts. Relating these measurements to the dimensions of the vocal tract of modern man and its sound-making capabilities, he fed the figures into a computer programed to calculate the resonances that corresponded to the range of shapes each vocal tract could have produced.

The results showed that the undeveloped pharynx would have prevented early man from making the quick shifts in pronunciation that modern man can; he would have been incapable of using the key vowels *a, i* and *u* in rapid combinations. Lieberman and Crelin concluded that early man would therefore have communicated verbally much more slowly than modern man—perhaps even as slowly as one tenth the speed we do.

This assessment of early man's limited facility in language is complemented by another theory addressed to an entirely different matter. Anthropologist Grover Krantz confronted a problem that has puzzled anthropologists for a long time: Why did the quality of Homo erectus' stone tools remain so static for so long? Over a period of thousands of years, no matter where found, they show little sign of improvement, as though all, somehow, had been made with the same models in mind. Why did they not become more sophisticated as time went on? Krantz has posed an ingenious explanation that sheds light on the acquisition of language by the first men. He suggests that Homo erectus' brain was not well enough developed to allow him to begin to speak until much later in his life than a child does today. And because Erectus was short-lived, he therefore had a shorter period in which to use his language to acquire and augment the skills necessary for toolmaking.

Krantz bases his conclusions about speech and toolmaking on studies of brain size. Taking a volume for the brain of 750 cubic centimeters as the dividing line between man and his predecessors, Krantz wondered why modern human brains should now average about 1,400 cubic centimeters, a 65 per cent increase over that of Homo erectus (which, in turn, was a 100 per cent increase over Australopithecus' brain size). In pondering that question, Krantz turned to the growth pattern of modern human brains. By the end of the first year of a baby's life, its brain reaches 750 cubic centimeters. This capacity, Krantz suggests, represents the threshold for speech; within half a year after that, the normal child begins to talk. Drawing a hypothetical curve of Homo erectus' brain development from infancy to childhood, Krantz showed that the 750 cubic centimeter size critical to speech may not have been achieved until after the sixth year. Prior to six, he argues, Homo erectus apparently did not have a big enough brain to be able to speak. His mental growth—if not his physical maturity—could have lagged about five years behind that of a modern human child. "When reproductive age was reached," Krantz theorizes, Homo erectus "had no more than seven years of cultural experience, whereas when the modern man reaches reproductive maturity he has at least 12 years of cultural experience. Age estimates of known fossil men indicate a very low life expectancy. . . . Five years would be an appreciable portion of the lives of most individuals. This shorter period of full cultural participation would limit the total quantity and complexity of cultural content that is likely to be transmitted in each generation."

But even with the speech limitations postulated by Krantz and Lieberman, Homo erectus would still have been able to communicate a great deal about himself and the world around him. It is necessary only to listen to very young children to see how effective language in its simplest form can be. Between the age of 18 and 24 months, only a half a year or so after a child says his first words, he begins to use two-word sentences. They are neither copies of grown-up speech nor reductions of it, but the child's own inventions, conforming to what would seem to be native, universal rules of grammar. They are made up of so-called open words—those that can be said by themselves and still mean something, such as "blanket," "milk" and "baby"—and pivot words, such as "on" and "hot." The child puts them together to describe the world or to get people to act ("pajama on"), but not to express emotion.

Only when the child is three or four does he consistently begin to put feelings into words. Before then he relies, as the nonhuman primates must, on the workings of the limbic system to call attention to his moods. Rather than say, "I'm angry," or "I'm afraid," he demonstrates physically how angry or afraid he is. He finds temper tantrums, whimpering or crying a much easier way to communicate; that is, he finds emotions easier to act out than to explain. As any parent knows, children have little difficulty in making themselves understood, and there is no reason to think that Homo erectus, speaking even the simplest of sentences, reinforced by gestures and hand signals, could not have communicated just as well with his early version of human speech.

Whatever it sounded like, and at whatever age he began to use it, the fact remains that Homo erectus had a language to use as a tool in its own right—a tool to drive like a wedge into the environment, hastening the split from nature that marked his development and foreshadowed ours. For the first time in human history cultural evolution began to outpace biological evolution as instinct and emotion were counterbalanced by custom and thought.

The Conquest of New Worlds to the North

Homo erectus was the first hominid to venture out of the tropics into the temperate world beyond. Over a period of a million years he spread in infinitely slow stages from Africa and Southeast Asia to the far ends of the Old World. The map below indicates the broad pathways he probably traced as he moved into new areas that offered water, food and the shelter of forests and caves. It also pinpoints some of the major sites in which his remains have been found. The pictures on the following pages suggest the look of the land in those far-flung places that Erectus is known to have passed through or visited, however briefly, and called home.

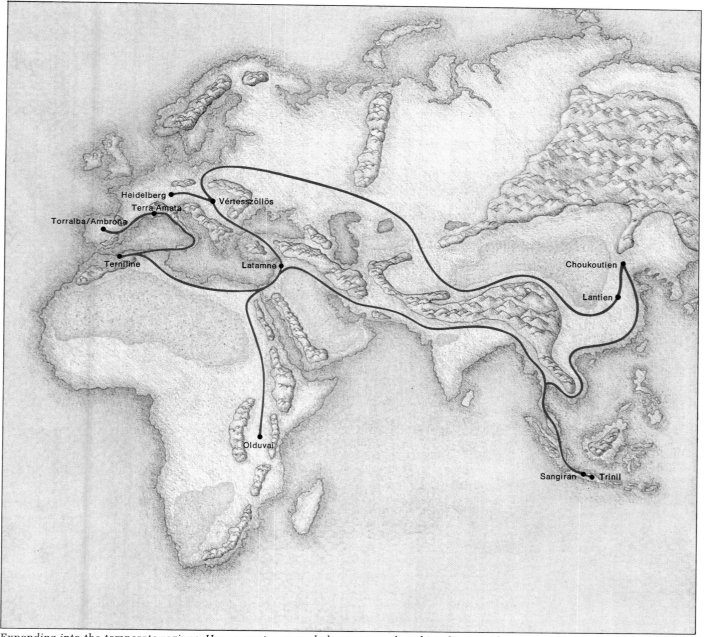

Expanding into the temperate regions, Homo erectus moved along routes that skirted natural barriers of mountains, sea and desert.

Streams, reed-fringed lakes and a warm climate offered Homo erectus hospitable campsites in his early East African homeland.

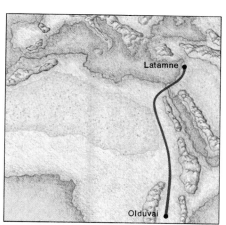

Like his Australopithecine ancestors,
Homo erectus lived throughout most of
tropical and subtropical Africa.
Perhaps the most famous of the African
sites where his remains have been
discovered is at Olduvai in Tanzania.
As man began expanding north into the
Eurasian continent, he probably moved
up the Nile River Valley and into
the Middle East; from such a place as
Latamne in northern Syria, where
Erectus artifacts have been found, the
way was open to both Asia and Europe.

Green hills and grazing land abounding with game invited hunters to northern Syria.

Rivers, whose banks provided natural campsites, and forests, which sheltered game, were two prominent features of the cool, well-watered country

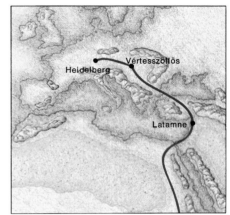

From the Middle East crossroads, the first men ranged across present-day Turkey into the Balkans, where river valleys provided access to Europe. Remains of Erectus have turned up at Vértesszöllös, Hungary; 450 miles to the northwest, in Germany, the famous Heidelberg man was found.

that Homo erectus settled in as he spread out slowly through the Balkans and into central Europe.

Finding scarce water, killing antelope and hyena, Erectus adapted even to the arid conditions of North Africa's rock-strewn hills.

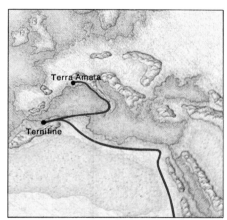

Some geologists think there may have been a land bridge spanning the Mediterranean from Tunis to Sicily and Italy during Homo erectus' time. If that were true, the first men could easily have moved from one side of the sea to the other, since they are known to have stopped at Ternifine in Algeria and Terra Amata near present-day Nice.

Limestone cliffs girded the northern Mediterranean beaches where Erectus camped.

Oak-clad mountains and valleys laced with streams provided good hunting grounds for Homo erectus in north-central Spain. There were also many

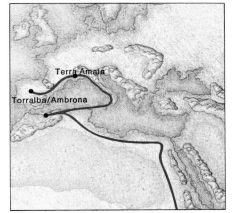

Scientists once thought that Homo erectus may have entered Spain from North Africa by a land bridge at Gibraltar, but now doubt that such a bridge existed. It is more likely that he moved down from southern France into central Spain, where he hunted at Torralba and Ambrona. Erectus probably followed the path of least resistance, going along the coast and skirting the Pyrenees to his west.

caves, which Erectus may have used in the harsh winters of a climate that was colder than it is now.

In north China, where Homo erectus spent thousands of centuries developing his hunting skills, the rich vegetation of open woodlands provided

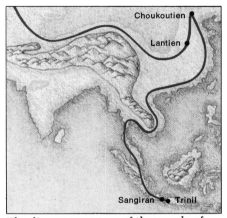

The distant ancestors of the people of Lantien and Choukoutien, near present-day Peking, may have made their way from Europe across the vast plains of Central Asia. It is more likely, however, that Homo erectus evolved in Southeast Asia, as he did in Africa, from Australopithecines, and then moved to the north. Java, where Homo erectus remains have been found at Trinil and Sangiran, must have been connected to the Malay Peninsula at certain times in geologic history.

good feed for the deer, buffalo and rhinoceros that the men there are known to have killed and eaten.

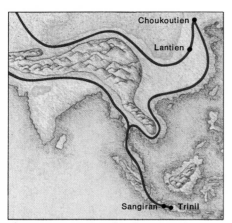

If Homo erectus evolved separately in tropical Southeast Asia and expanded along the Malay Peninsula up into China, he probably spread north and west as well. The expansion would have taken him into India, where Erectus probably settled at an early date, or where he may have even evolved. The first men may also have continued west, passing south of the Himalaya mountains—perhaps at the same time as other men were moving toward them from the Middle East.

In the Southeast Asia of Erectus' day, volcanoes towered above the clouds that hung over the river

valleys and blanketed the lower slopes of the mountains each morning. Bamboo grew thick in swamps along the rivers, and forests covered the hills.

The social patterns that shape human lives today were first woven by the men and women who camped on the sandy beach of Terra Amata, who hunted in the chilly hills around Torralba and Ambrona, who lived for so many generations in the sooty caves of Choukoutien. In these and countless other undiscovered places in the temperate regions where Homo erectus settled half a million years ago, he established many of the paths that the genus Homo would follow until the present.

These great innovations, which forever set man apart from his animal ancestors, are clearly linked to the decisive turn to hunting as a way of life and Erectus' equally dramatic expansion into temperate regions of the Old World. Each influenced the other.

The move from the tropics was perhaps the high adventure of those million years during which Homo erectus was establishing man as nature's dominant figure. Before the great expansion, his immediate ancestors had been evolving much as the other animals around them were, adapting imperceptibly to their environment, using some tools in a primitive way, living in loose social groups, depending on a generally benign environment for food and warmth, having very little awareness of the past or thought for the future. But when Erectus moved out into the world's previously unpeopled regions, this way of life began to alter. By meeting the challenges of changing con-

How the family, the basic unit of human society, became established in the Homo erectus band is indicated in this diagrammatic sketch. All members of the band were related, as shown by their shared basic color, but they presumably split into loosely bonded subgroups, identified by color shading. These first families were formed as a woman came to depend on a hunting man for meat, while he depended on her for foraged food; their helpless infants depended on both.

ditions with solutions of his own making, rather than waiting until evolution did it for him, man passed a crucial milestone: for the first time, a creature, however unconsciously, took an active hand in its own evolution. It was the beginning of man's supremacy, and it was the most significant contribution Homo erectus made to human development.

Homo erectus' move into new territory was a perfectly natural occurrence—if a development that took nearly a million years can be called an occurrence. All living things, from bacteria to whales, multiply and spread into all areas to which they can adapt; Australopithecines certainly moved east and west throughout as much of the Old World tropics as they could get to. But just as surely as whales' limits are defined by the shores of their oceans, so Australopithecus was stymied by his inability to adapt to the environmental barriers at the edges of the subtropics. Homo erectus prevailed over these obstacles not because he developed any new bodily equipment but because he had a better brain.

Clearly the temperate world was a more difficult place to live in than the tropics. First there was the seasonal variation in the vegetable food supply—during cold or dry seasons, fruits, berries and edible shoots were hard to find. Hunting, which had been important to man in the tropics, became immeasurably more so as a means of tiding him over when vegetable foods were sparse. Dependence on hunting in turn demanded more efficient techniques and more complex social organization. Furthermore, many of the creatures Erectus hunted were different from those in the tropics, and their habits and weaknesses had to be learned.

Just as big a problem for man, particularly as he moved farther north, was the faint sunlight of winters and the cold itself, which varied not only with latitude and the season but also with the ice age fluctuations. At best the cold was uncomfortable; at worst, when the ice caps moved down out of the north, it could be fatal, and man had to find a way to fight it. Hominids had evolved the efficient system of perspiration to prevent overheating in the tropics, but had not needed to develop a counterbalancing system equally effective against overcooling, and naked, sweat-chilled skin was no help in the cold.

In time, a few adaptations to extreme cold were to appear among humans, but in Homo sapiens rather than Homo erectus. It was hundreds of thousands of years later in human history before the Eskimos acquired compact body structure to conserve internal warmth. Such changes require a long time to evolve, but Erectus did not need to wait for them to cope with the cold: he was intelligent enough to deal with the problem without depending on evolution—he generated extra heat with fire, put on hide clothes and took shelter in caves.

One physical change that apparently did come about in response to Erectus' exploration of northern lands was associated less with cold than with the scarcity of sunlight during winter in the higher latitudes. Human skin probably got lighter. Scientific opinion is not unanimous on this point, but it seems likely that Australopithecus, as well as early, tropical Erectus, had been quite dark-skinned. In equatorial Africa, the dark color was an advantage. The ultraviolet rays of the tropical sun are harmful to skin, and many experts feel that as the hominids' skin became less hairy and more exposed, the melanocytes—the cells that produce skin-darkening pigment—compensated by producing extra pigment to block the ultraviolet rays.

But pigment also inhibits the synthesis of vitamin D in the skin. This diminution of vitamin production is not a serious problem in the tropics, where there is so much sun that enough is made anyway; when man settled permanently in regions with less sunlight, however, he did not get enough vitamin D—particularly since he was now wearing animal hides—and pigment was no longer a protection but a drawback. In these conditions, skin that could contribute vitamin D to the body's chemistry was better for survival, and so lighter skin evolved. There are some questions about this theory. Why are not all peoples native to the tropics dark-skinned? Why did some African jungle tribes, who live in shade, become so dark? Why did the bushmen, who live in the desert sun, develop yellowish, rather than black, skins? Yet mankind's skin color did become differentiated at some point, and it seems likely to have happened first in Homo erectus' day.

A far more significant change in Homo erectus at this time was the increase in his brain size. Even before he began to move out of the tropics his brain had far outgrown that of his predecessors, but the process of growth appears to have speeded up in the crisis of adjusting to new conditions. A skull fragment from the Erectus site at Vértesszöllös, Hungary, indicates a cranial capacity of about 1,400 cubic centimeters—larger than the mean for modern man. The largest Erectus cranium yet found in tropical Africa, by contrast, measures 1,000 cubic centimeters. This comparison may well be misleading, since the African skull is a great deal older than the other, and since the very few Erectus skulls that have been found cannot possibly tell the whole story; more skulls may be discovered that will lessen the apparent discrepancy. Still, it seems reasonable that the demands of a rigorous new environment could have spurred the development of a trend that was so obviously an advantage to survival.

However it happened, the growth of man's brain had a paradoxical corollary that was fundamental to man's social development: the bigger and more complex his brain grew, the more helpless he became at birth. Compared with other mammals, which emerge from the womb almost fully developed, ready to stand on their own or cling to their mothers, man seems like a creature born before he is ready—in a condition, as anthropologist Loren Eiseley has put it, of "peculiar larval nakedness."

A baby horse can get to its feet within two hours, and after a day can run along with its mother. Among apes and monkeys the infant has big toes that enable it to hang on to its mother's fur. Within a day or two, a baboon baby, for example, can cling unaided to its mother's hair while she moves around in search of food and water; within 12 months the baboon is more or less on its own. The human baby, by contrast, is utterly dependent on his mother. He has to be carried and supplied with almost all his needs for at least two years; it may be six years before he is as able to take care of himself as a baboon is at 12 months.

Clearly the human infant enters the world much earlier in his development than other animals, at a stage in which his brain is still too unformed to let him walk and forage for himself. The reason he is born before his brain is ready is an intriguing one that is directly related to the size of the human brain.

During birth, the baby must pass from the womb through a bony ring in the mother's pelvis; since the head is the biggest part of the baby, the size of the pelvis limits the size of the infant's head. During the evolution of Homo erectus, the brain and head were increasing in size much faster, proportionately, than was his body—or the female pelvis; the pelvis, in fact, could not have grown much more without making upright running difficult for females. Were the baby's head to have achieved full or even half growth in the womb, neither mother nor child could have survived the birth. Evolution's solution to the dilemma was to produce a creature whose brain would do most of its growing outside the womb.

The modern human brain at birth is only 25 per cent of its adult size. By contrast, the brain of the newborn chimpanzee is 65 per cent. It has been estimated that an Australopithecine infant entered the world with 40 or 50 per cent brain development; and that in Homo erectus the infant brain development had been reduced to about 30 per cent.

Once outside the womb, this brain of the first men grew to a comparatively prodigious size, and it was a new kind of brain; a brain in which intellect outweighed instinct, in which learning, unique in each individual, superseded genetic programming; a brain whose potential was seemingly inversely proportional to its initial helplessness. But oddly, this initial helplessness was equally important to the progress of mankind. Because it made the baby totally dependent on his mother for so long, it molded a social structure that was to become uniquely man's.

One measure of a society's development is the extent to which its different parts must rely on one another for the whole to function. As Homo erectus

The Helpless Infant

HUMAN CHILD

AGE	CHARACTERISTIC BEHAVIOR	PER CENT OF ADULT BRAIN SIZE
AT BIRTH	Depends completely on mother for food, transportation and protection Exhibits grasping reflex: automatically grabs an object that touches his palm Stretches arms outward, then together over his chest, in a grasping gesture, when his head falls backward	25 per cent
3 MONTHS	Raises his head when lying down, supporting his weight on his forearms Turns body from back to side Vocalizes through cooing	35 per cent
6 MONTHS	Sits up unsupported Exhibits coordination: reaches purposefully for an object and grasps it Vocalizes through babbling one-syllable sounds	45 per cent
9 MONTHS	Stands upright when supported Crawls on all fours Takes a few steps holding on to an adult	50 per cent
1 YEAR	Stands upright and walks unsupported Responds more to play objects than to playmates Responds to verbal commands and says first words	60 per cent
2 YEARS	Runs upright Moves quickly from sitting to standing position Uses a cup as a drinking tool Plays as much with playmates as with play objects Exhibits great interest in stacking objects in tower formation Speaks with a vocabulary of more than 50 words and uses two-word sentences	70 per cent
4 YEARS	Actively practices motor skills: running, jumping, hopping Plays extensively with other children Has the ability to understand and use language with precision	80 per cent
8 TO 9 YEARS	Learns to cooperate with others and masters control over impulses and aggression within a group Thinks in abstract terms and exhibits great interest in solving problems	95 per cent
12 TO 14 YEARS (PUBERTY)	Exhibits increasing interest in the opposite sex	100 per cent

Paradoxically, although Homo erectus developed a bigger brain than his ancestors, he was born more helpless than they, with proportionally less of his brain developed. It did most of its growing after birth, thus giving him a long time in which to learn before maturing. How this slow start helped win the race can be seen by comparing the behavior and brain growth of a modern child—like Homo erectus, slow to mature—with those of a chimpanzee (charts above and opposite), man's closest primate relative. The agility, growth and learning abilities of a modern child advance about one third slower than a chimp's during the first year of life. But by the age of four or five the child has largely completed learning language—a talent a chimp never acquires.

CHIMPANZEE

AGE	CHARACTERISTIC BEHAVIOR	PER CENT OF ADULT BRAIN SIZE
AT BIRTH	Depends completely on mother for food, transportation and protection Exhibits grasping reflex: clings to its mother's chest with hands and feet Stretches arms outward, then together over its chest in a grasping gesture	65 per cent
3 MONTHS	Sits up unsupported Exhibits coordination: reaches purposefully for an object and grasps it	70 per cent
6 MONTHS	Stands upright when supported Moves about on all fours Takes a few steps holding on to an adult	70 per cent
9 MONTHS	Stands upright and walks unsupported Actively swings through trees, leaping from branch to branch Plays with other young chimpanzees	70 per cent
1 YEAR	Runs upright and on all fours	70 per cent
2 YEARS	Engages in social activities with chimps of all ages except infants	75 per cent
4 YEARS	Completely independent of mother for food and transportation Plays much of day with other chimps and its mother Makes and uses tools to obtain food and drink Begins to vocalize using noises to express fear, excitement, anticipation of food and pleasure during grooming	85 per cent
8 TO 9 YEARS (PUBERTY)	Spends increasing amount of time in social grooming and in feeding itself as it devotes less time to play Begins sexual interest and activity	100 per cent

The chimp starts out life way ahead of man: such powers as it achieves, it achieves relatively early. At one year of age, the chimp has the mental capacity of a year-old child, but the motor skills of a four-year-old and the strength of an eight-year-old. By the age of two, its play behavior resembles that of a human: both are learning about the world by toying with objects and socializing with companions of the same age. But although the chimp learns some meaningful sounds and can be taught to communicate fairly well with symbols and sign language, it lacks the brain "wiring" and vocal apparatus needed for talking. And so, although its brain is nearly three quarters as large at birth as it is at puberty, it never grows wiser than a five-year-old human.

evolved, the links of dependence among individuals strengthened and became more numerous—babies depended upon mothers, youngsters upon adults, hunter upon hunter, men and women upon each other, eventually group upon group. These relationships were almost certainly forged by the first men; further steps toward civilization—development of clans, tribes, races—did not come until many thousands of years after Erectus became Sapiens.

The infant's dependence on his mother must have forced an enormous change in his parent's habits. The baby baboon, hanging on to its mother's fur, hardly hampers her at all; she is still able to keep up with the troop as it makes its daily rounds for food and water. She feeds herself and her infant. There is no sharing of effort, no storing of food, and nursing mothers are on their own along with everyone else. Human babies, on the other hand, had to be carried by their mothers, or by someone, and held while nursing—a nursing mother would have had a hard time keeping up with the men on their hunting forays. So as meat became more and more important in their diet, the women would have become more and more dependent on the men to supply it for them.

But men needed women just as much. Hunting, for all its importance to early man, was not an easy way of life, and the hunt was by no means an infallible source of food. In fact, it is likely that early man worked a good deal harder to get enough to eat than did his simian relatives. Baboons find ample sustenance by wandering through the trees and grass of an area that seldom covers more than three to six square miles, and gorillas support themselves within a range of 15 square miles. Homo erectus had to cover far more territory to find his food. It has been estimated

that it took as much as 10 square miles to support a single hunter—a band of 30 people would have ranged over an area of 300 square miles in supplying itself with meat. And hunters then were less sure of making a kill every time they went out than modern hunters are. Even if an Erectus group made out as well as primitive hunting tribes do today, the kills probably provided no more than a fourth of the food the band needed to live on. The rest had to be supplied by the women. It was they, gathering nuts, fruits, roots and berries, who kept the group alive.

This male-female interdependence, peculiar to man among the primates, must have begun to develop several million years before Homo erectus' day, when hominids first moved onto the open savanna and started making meat an important source of food. It seems reasonable to suppose that the males, stronger and faster than the females, would gradually have concentrated more and more on hunting, while the women, hampered by dependent babies, would have become responsible for the gathering.

By the time of Homo erectus, when hunters were tackling larger and more dangerous prey, bigger game required more hunters working together, and the specialization of work had become more definitive. The division of labor between men and women, which is accepted—or challenged—in today's culture as a traditional social arrangement, had by then become essential to survival. Men and women separately on an every-individual-for-himself basis would almost certainly have starved; working together in distinct roles as hunters and foragers, they formed a successful economic team.

While hunting was forging a new male-female relationship and large brain size was altering the infant-mother relationship, still another relationship—male to female to young—was developing. This three-way interdependence was perhaps most important of all, for it was to become the basic unit of human society, the family. Family living is one of the few characteristics that can be singled out as unique to man. It does not exist in the same form among animals, even among such intelligent primates as chimpanzees. Among humans it exists today in one version or another everywhere on earth and clearly has existed since long before recorded history. Whether it was first organized by Homo erectus is arguable, yet it is so fundamental to human life that a creature worthy of the name Homo can hardly be imagined outside a family setting.

A very crude forerunner of the human family can be traced back to the Australopithecines. Interdependence and some division of labor began to appear in their time, fostering very impermanent relationships among subgroups of men and women within the band. By Homo erectus' day, these subdivisions were becoming clearly established. If an Erectus band encompassed 20 to 50 individuals, as most experts believe, it included perhaps three to a dozen prototype family units.

It is tempting to think of these closely related subgroups as traditional Western families—Mom, Dad and the children making up a tightly knit unit of their own. But all sorts of human families exist today and the European or American nuclear type is not the most common (or even, in reality, the only one popular in Europe and the United States). The earliest families may have evolved under the leadership of the father, the mother or the uncle (all these systems are to be found today) and may have included several females for a male or several males for a female. What is common to all types of families is three-way interdependence. One or a few males assume some measure of special responsibility for one or a few females and their children, while the females owe special duties to the males and children, and the children feel a special commitment to their own elders.

This interdependence is a matter of degree, more noticeable now than in its early form when individuals often shifted or even shared allegiance among family units, probably more easily than they do now, and children in particular tended to be viewed as the charge of an entire band rather than of their families alone. Yet by Erectus' day the ties that distinguish families within a society must have been growing markedly stronger, for they seem to be associated with sexual habits and mate-selection practices that also developed at this time and have come to help distinguish humans from their animal relatives.

The compelling factor in apes' and monkeys' sex habits is the females' estrus, or heat; their sexual responsiveness is controlled by hormones and flares up and dies down with measured regularity. During the brief estrus, female nonhuman primates encourage the males to copulate with them, and they often mate with several males one after another—even those they normally would ignore.

During hominid evolution, this estrus cycle gradually became modified so that humans became capable of year-round sexual receptivity. Thus the periodic frenzy and promiscuity that governed—and still govern—the nonhuman primates' sex lives no longer occurred. Men and women could exert control over their sexual behavior, and could decide when —and with whom—they mated. This physical change

Evolving Social Contacts

While Homo erectus moved out geographically from the tropics to temperate regions, he was also moving out socially from isolation within a homogeneous band to ever-broadening contacts with other people and other bands. He formed the social patterns that ultimately led to modern relationships among humans.

Before Erectus' day, his ancestor Australopithecus lived in an inbred, self-sufficient group (right) that lacked any special organization. But its members eventually began to divide up the daily work, a specialization of role that was to be carried on by Erectus and lead to family life and changes in sex habits. Promiscuity and incest became less common, so mates were selected from outside the family, and eventually from outside the band itself. It was this intermarriage between bands, called exogamy, that helped Erectus bands to begin cooperating with one another (opposite, top).

Group cooperation was becoming necessary as Erectus relied more and more on hunting. A single band contained too few active men to bring off large-scale hunts, such as the trapping of elephants at Torralba-Ambrona in Spain (pages 78-79). Evidence found there indicates that two or three bands, presumably related, joined forces year after year for the elephant hunt. But such cooperation was informal and infrequent until Homo erectus was replaced by Homo sapiens. By then populations had grown and the value of cooperation was so firmly established that many bands grouped together on a more or less regular basis to form a clan (opposite, bottom) —and the foundations of human society had been laid.

1 | **An Australopithecine group** needed no contact with others. It was a small unit of about 15 individuals, and because mating was promiscuous, everyone was closely related—as indicated by the single color—and there were no clearly defined family subunits. The group was self-sufficient: Australopithecus subsisted on vegetation and easily caught small prey that members could collect by themselves.

2 | **Homo erectus bands** probably developed contacts with one another based on exogamy, or outbreeding; the two facing groups shown here are independent but each includes members from the other (indicated by the two different colors) who were brought in as mates. These kinship ties would encourage the bands to cooperate in hunting that required a large number of men, such as attacking elephants.

3 | **Homo sapiens bands** extended their contacts to incorporate many groups—for hunting, rituals or simply socializing—but the basis for these allegiances remained the kinship ties indicated by the colors and shadings in the drawing. The four bands shown are made up of descendants of two families, represented by blue and green, and the closeness of relationship is suggested by the intensity of color.

2

3

led to what the anthropologist Bernard Campbell has called "the individualization of sex." Couples could now become partners.

This mating probably was not permanent, or even monogamous, particularly if there were more men than women in the band (or vice versa). Furthermore, since hunting was communal, the sharing of food probably was also, so that a man would not have been expected to provide all the meat a particular woman needed. Nevertheless, it seems inescapable that certain men and women would have attracted each other and formed some sort of liaison that they, and the group, recognized as binding. They would have bedded down together, kept company when the band was on the move, and paid particular attention to each other's needs. In addition, a man would have taken a parental interest in the children of the woman he favored, even if he did not specifically recognize them as his own issue; the boys would have gone on hunting forays with the men as soon as they were strong enough to keep up, and the men would have formed close ties with their protégés as they initiated them into the skills and arts of the hunt.

Kinship ties in the group would almost certainly have been extended by the presence of a few grandparents—men and women who were past their hunting and child-bearing days but who were honored for their skills at toolmaking or teaching—or valued simply as baby-sitters. The continuity of genetic lines would thus be emphasized, and family patterns would have taken on a firmer definition.

As these family patterns became etched deeper into the emerging society, there was undoubtedly a more marked avoidance of incest. These inhibitions are evident in some of the apes and monkeys: among Japanese macaques, for instance, there is apparently some sort of restraint against sex between mother and son, and in chimpanzees this inhibition is usually extended to include brother and sister, although in general chimps are entirely promiscuous in their sex lives. In modern man the taboo against incest is almost universal; sometime during the evolution of early men, then, the partial inhibition became the hard and fast taboo. It seems fair to suggest that as Erectus grew more aware of kinship structures within his community a disinclination toward sex within the family group became more pronounced.

Erectus' tendency to look afield for mates grew, and eventually he reached beyond his own band to select a partner from a neighboring group. This practice, which anthropologists call exogamy, certainly would have had advantages. Speech would have enabled Homo erectus to symbolize family relationships, and the development of blood ties between neighbors would have encouraged intergroup harmony. When bands with common boundaries are related, a practice of sharing develops—when game becomes scarce the bands hunt freely over one another's territory.

Exogamy, by bringing in mates strange to the band, presumably made family ties ever more important. With that importance came another cultural innovation, one that seems elemental but was a milestone in society's growth: the idea of a home base.

It is all very well for apes to travel everywhere, always, as a group; each individual does its own foraging, and the safety of the individual lies in the numbers of the group. But 24-hour togetherness simply would not have worked for Homo erectus, whose hunters ranged so far and whose young were such a burden. The solution was a base camp—a place, however temporary, where the children could be looked after and the fires kept burning, where the women could stock-pile the fruits of their gathering and to which the men could return after a day or two on the hunt. Apparently two kinds of home developed—one temporary, one permanent.

If the hunters were following migrating animals, the bases were used only as long as the animals were in the area, as at Terra Amata; even there, the visitors saw fit to build huts for shelter each time they came—and the 11 huts, apparently built in consecutive years on the same sand dune, suggest a group with a well-ordered annual schedule and perhaps even a feeling of attachment for a favored spot. It is almost possible to visualize youngsters, running ahead of the band as it approaches the sea, eagerly looking to see if last year's house is still standing.

Choukoutien was not a temporary home. There, where in one cave layers of hearth ashes were found to be 22 feet thick, the base must have been more or less permanent: no doubt it was in a favored location where water and game were within close range.

No other primate society incorporates either permanent or temporary bases, although other animals mark off ranges of territory they regard as peculiarly their own. Most apes show a preference for certain clumps of trees within their territories for sleeping in; the Hamadryas baboons of Ethiopia have been observed to gather, 700 strong, to spend the night together on a rocky cliff that offers protection while they sleep. In the morning the animals split up into smaller groups; each group stays together on its rounds, and where the group goes, all go.

With a home base, man had a new social blueprint. For one thing, the existence of a home meant that sick or infirm individuals no longer faced abandonment along the way; now there was a place where they could rest and mend in comparative safety. "For a wild primate," the anthropologists Sherwood Washburn and Irven DeVore have written, "a fatal sickness is one that separates it from the troop, but for man it is one from which he cannot recover even while protected and fed at the home base. . . . It is the home base that changes sprained ankles and fevers from fatal diseases to minor ailments."

Thus the invention of home must have affected the normal death rate; still, only a few Homo erectus individuals are believed to have attained the age of 40, and anyone who survived until 50 would have reached a ripe old age indeed. Most died much earlier, as is shown by poignant evidence from the caves at Choukoutien: 50 per cent of the human bones found belonged to children under 14 years of age.

In terms of man's society the real importance of the home base was that it provided a medium for man's cultural growth. Within the safe circle of its carefully tended fire grew a fellowship, a sense of community that was new on earth. The hearth nurtured self-awareness and trust among individuals in a world that was otherwise largely ruled by nature's fang and claw. There man could begin to learn more than simply how to survive; he could grapple with concepts, fashion a language, improve his tools and weapons, conceive new ways to change the world.

The home, for all it contributed to human growth, may also be involved in another, and much less desirable, hallmark of human society—one that some observers think they can trace to the first men and beyond. That is modern man's unhappy tendency to wreak violence on his own kind. Author Robert Ardrey, for example, has hypothesized that man instinctively guards whatever territory he considers his own and will defend it violently, if necessary, against all comers. Other writers and scientists suggest that an innate propensity for aggression, carried over from animal forebears, explains all man's violent behavior from wars to riots to throwing dishes in a domestic quarrel. For example, Konrad Lorenz, the Austrian authority on animal behavior, argues that this innate drive will always express itself forcibly one way or another; if it is not channeled productively, in society's terms, it will burst out destructively—sooner or later, but inevitably.

Most anthropologists today, however, disagree with this view, believing that there is no specific aggressive drive innate in man, but merely the potential for this kind of behavior, and that this potential is shaped by society. For instance, when a man is threatened, or thinks he is threatened, by another, his unaffected response might just as well be to flee the threat as to fight the provoker. His culture determines which response it should be.

David Pilbeam, an anthropologist at Yale, believes that aggressive behavior is unnatural not only in man but also in the monkeys and the apes. "The degree to which such behavior is developed," he postulates, "depends very considerably indeed upon cultural values and learning. Territoriality, likewise, is not a 'natural' feature of human group living; nor is it among most other primates."

This analysis is borne out by observation of several hunting-gathering peoples living today, such as the Kung bushmen of the Kalahari desert in southern Africa. The bushmen are not particularly territory-minded, and among themselves are markedly unaggressive, regarding hospitality and generosity as normal. Even more mild are the Tasaday people discovered living in Stone Age primitiveness in the Philippine jungle (pages 137-147). These quiet, gentle people live in harmony with their surroundings and apparently exhibit no driving aggressiveness in any aspect of their society.

Homo erectus, too, must have been a peaceable creature. He lived by the club and spear, it is true, but only to feed himself and his kin. Sharing of food was basic to his existence, and since his possessions were limited by the kind of life he led, covetousness and greed could hardly have driven Homo erectus to violence. Yet the possibility of conflict between Erectus bands cannot be entirely eliminated—the skulls of Choukoutien suggesting cannibalism have not really been explained.

Such hostilities, if they occurred, must have been rare and unplanned in an uncrowded world in which there were no natural examples of creatures systematically setting upon their own kind. It appears likely that war, covetousness, greed and cruelty were later developments, coming after man settled down on the land, became more numerous and forged cultures that encouraged individual and group pride in possessions, territories and beliefs, even as they fostered art, science and humanity.

These are today's problems, and there is little reason to think they much afflicted Homo erectus. He was taking on his own challenges and, with perseverance and imagination, solving them remarkably well. To his success we owe our flaws and triumphs.

Present-Day Reminders of Earliest Man

On the slope of a jungle mountain on the Philippine island of Mindanao exists a fragile link with Homo erectus. There, in deep isolation, lives a band of people called the Tasaday; their primitive existence resembles the pattern of the earliest Stone Age.

Although too close a comparison is not justifiable—the Tasaday are, after all, Homo sapiens, and are therefore modern in an evolutionary sense —many of their cultural adaptations are similar to those attributed to their ancient human ancestors. The Tasaday make and use stone tools; their group numbers about 25, just as Erectus bands did; they are dependent on fires for survival, and they lead a hunting-foraging life that closely resembles that of the first true men.

Because their needs are few and nature is indulgent, they never want and they are always ready to share with one another—a characteristic also attributed to Erectus. But the Tasaday display some traits of their own. They seem unable to remember much further back than five or six years, yet they revere the philosophy of their ancestors; following it, they choose to live together in a cave, to care for the trees and rocks around it—and to stay close to their isolated home.

Four Tasaday relax at the entrance to their cave home, 450 feet up the slope of an 800-foot mountain. The name of their band is taken from the angular peak in which the cave is located.

Dressed in orchid leaves and smudged by ashes from their fires, members of the Tasaday band relax outside their home. The cave has a 30-foot-wide entrance and contains a chamber 25 to 40 feet deep. It is undecorated but is regularly swept with split bamboo brooms. Two fires are kept burning —the Tasaday, like Erectus, never let the flames die. At night they remain inside, fearful of snakes; when they go out in search of the day's food shortly after sunrise, they seldom venture more than two miles from the cave.

◄ In a scene as old as man (left), a mother comforts her child. The intimate bonds among the Tasaday and their close living quarters have made children a concern of everyone, as presumably they were in Erectus' day; if a parent dies, the group helps rear the child.

A Tasaday woman and two children ► wash off the soot from the cave fires in the stream that flows at the base of their hill. When anthropologists first visited the band in 1971, thirteen of its members, more than half, were children—all but two of them boys.

Fire is as precious to the Tasaday as it was to Homo erectus. No one knows if the first men could start a flame or simply preserved natural fire, but the Tasaday are adept fire makers, using an ancient device called a fire drill. In these photographs a man twirls a stick between his palms until a drill hole in the base board heats up, then dried palm bark and moss are applied (opposite, top). As the tinder ignites, the fire maker blows on it (right)—and all faces light up as flames appear. The process takes about five minutes.

Fishing is a communal job; a boy holds leaf cones in which the men's catch—made barehanded—will be kept and eventually cooked.

Probing under rocks, men hunt tadpoles, a major source of animal protein for the Tasaday. Crabs and fish are also highly prized.

Starch is provided by a variety of wild yam, here being washed. Later the yam will be roasted in the hot coals of the cave fires.

The Tasaday spend their days together, and since their
chores and diversions are few, they often sit in silent, closely
knit groups, as Homo erectus is believed to have done.
Having learned to cooperate, they are secure in their
relationships with one another. They are monogamous and
never divorce, although there are more men in the band
than women. As was probably the case with the earliest
men, the Tasaday have no headman, and no serious rivalries
—each does what he does best and decisions are based on
consensus. Being thus at peace with one another and in
harmony with their environment, the Tasaday were
described by an anthropologist, who observed their quiet
ways, as among "the gentlest people on the face of the earth."

The Emergence of Man

This chart records the progression of life on earth from its first appearance in the waters of the new-formed planet through the evolution of man; it traces his physical, social, technological and intellectual development to the Christian era. To place these advances in commonly used chronological sequences, the column

Left Panel

Geology	Archeology	Billions of Years Ago	
Precambrian earliest era		4.5	Creation of the Earth
		4	Formation of the primordial sea
			First life, single-celled algae and bacteria, appears in water
		3	
		2	
		1	
		Millions of Years Ago	
			First oxygen-breathing animals appear
		800	
Paleozoic ancient life			Primitive organisms develop interdependent specialized cells
		600	Shell-bearing multicelled invertebrate animals appear
			Evolution of armored fish, first animals to possess backbones
		400	Small amphibians venture onto land
			Reptiles and insects arise
			Thecodont, ancestor of dinosaurs, arises
Mesozoic middle life			Age of dinosaurs begins
		200	Birds appear
			Mammals live in shadow of dinosaurs
			Age of dinosaurs ends
		80	
			Prosimians, earliest primates, develop in trees
Cenozoic recent life		60	
		40	Monkeys and apes evolve
		20	
		10	Ramapithecus, oldest known primate with apparently manlike traits, evolves in India and Africa
		8	
		6	Australopithecus, closest primate ancestor to man, appears in Africa
		4	

Right Panel

Geology	Archeology	Millions of Years Ago	
Lower Pleistocene oldest period of most recent epoch	**Lower Paleolithic** oldest period of Old Stone Age	2	Oldest known tool fashioned by man in Africa
			First true man, Homo erectus, emerges in East Indies and Africa
		1	Homo erectus migrates throughout Old World tropics
		Thousands of Years Ago	
Middle Pleistocene middle period of most recent epoch		800	Homo erectus populates temperate zones
			Man learns to control and use fire
		600	
			Large-scale, organized elephant hunts staged in Europe
		400	Man begins to make artificial shelters from branches
		200	
Upper Pleistocene latest period of most recent epoch	**Middle Paleolithic** middle period of Old Stone Age		Neanderthal man emerges in Europe
		80	
		60	Ritual burials in Europe and Near East suggest belief in afterlife
			Woolly mammoths hunted by Neanderthals in northern Europe
			Cave bear becomes focus of cult in Europe
		40	
	Upper Paleolithic latest period of Old Stone Age	30	Cro-Magnon man arises in Europe
			Man reaches Australia
			Oldest known written record, a lunar calendar on bone, made in Europe
			Asian hunters cross Bering Strait to populate North and South America
			Figurines sculpted for nature worship
			First artists decorate walls and ceilings of caves in France and Spain
		20	Invention of needle makes sewing possible
			Bison hunting begins on Great Plains of North America
Holocene present epoch	**Mesolithic** Middle Stone Age	10	Bow and arrow invented in Europe
			Dog domesticated in North America

(Last Ice Age spans the Upper Pleistocene through Holocene in the Geology column)

▼ Four billion years ago

▼ Three billion years ago

▲ Origin of the Earth (4.5 billion)

▲ First life (3.5 billion)

at the far left of each of the chart's four sections identifies the great geological eras into which earth history is divided, while the second column lists the archeological ages of human history. The key dates in the rise of life and of man's outstanding accomplishments appear in the third column (years and events mentioned in this volume of

The Emergence of Man appear in bold type). The chart is not to scale; the reason is made clear by the bar below, which represents in linear scale the 4.5 billion years spanned by the chart—on the scaled bar, the portion relating to the total period of known human existence (far right) is too small to be distinguished.

Geology	Archeology	Years B.C.	
Holocene (cont.)	Mesolithic (cont.)	9000	Jericho settled as the first town
			Sheep domesticated in Near East
	Neolithic New Stone Age		
		8000	Pottery first made in Japan
			Goat domesticated in Persia
			Man cultivates his first crops, wheat and barley, in Near East
		7000	Pattern of village life grows in Near East
			Catal Huyuk, in what is now Turkey, becomes the first trading center
			Loom invented in Near East
			Agriculture begins to replace hunting in Europe
		6000	Cattle domesticated in Near East
			Copper used in trade in Mediterranean area
	Copper Age		Corn cultivated in Mexico
		4000	Sail-propelled boats used in Egypt
			Oldest known massive stone monument built in Brittany
			First cities rise on plains of Sumer
			Cylinder seals begin to be used as marks of identification in Near East
		3500	First potatoes grown in South America
			Wheel originates in Sumer
			Egyptian merchant trading ships start to ply the Mediterranean
			First writing, pictographic, composed, Near East
		3000	Bronze first used to make tools in Near East
	Bronze Age		City life spreads to Nile Valley
			Plow is developed in Near East
			Accurate calendar based on stellar observation devised in Egypt
			Sumerians invent potter's wheel
			Silk moth domesticated in China
			Minoan navigators begin to venture into seas beyond the Mediterranean
		2600	Variety of gods and heroes glorified in Gilgamesh and other epics in Near East
			Pyramids built in Egypt
		2500	Cities rise in the Indus Valley

Geology	Archeology	Years B.C.	
Holocene (cont.)	Bronze Age (cont.)	2400	Stonehenge, most famous of ancient stone monuments, begun in England
			Earliest written code of laws drawn up in Sumer
		2000	Chicken and elephant domesticated in Indus Valley
			Use of bronze spreads to Europe
			Eskimo culture begins in Bering Strait area
			Man begins to cultivate rice in Far East
			Herdsmen of Central Asia learn to tame and ride horses
		1500	Invention of ocean-going outrigger canoes enables man to reach islands of South Pacific
			Oldest known paved roads built in Crete
			Ceremonial bronze sculptures created in China
			Imperial government, ruling distant provinces, established by Hittites
	Iron Age	1400	Iron in use in Near East
			First complete alphabet devised in script of the Ugarit people in Syria
			Hebrews introduce concept of monotheism
		1000	Reindeer domesticated in northern Europe
		900	Phoenicians develop modern alphabet
		800	Celtic culture begins to spread use of iron throughout Europe
			Nomads create a far-flung society based on the horse in Russian steppes
			First highway system built in Assyria
			Homer composes Iliad and Odyssey
		700	Rome founded
			Wheel barrow invented in China
		200	Epics about India's gods and heroes, the Mahabharata and Ramayana, written
			Water wheel invented in Near East
		0	Christian era begins

▼ Two billion years ago

▼ One billion years ago

First oxygen-breathing animals (900 million) ▲

First animals to possess ▲
backbones (470 million)

First men (1.3 million) ▲

Credits

The sources for illustrations in this book are shown below. Credits from left to right are separated by semicolons, from top to bottom by dashes.

Cover—Painting by Burt Silverman, background photograph from ENTHEOS. 8 —Painting by Burt Silverman, background photograph by Richard Jeffery. 10 through 17 —Paintings by Roger Hane. 23 through 31 —Paintings by David Leffel, background photographs are listed separately; 23—Pete Turner. 24,25—Dick Swanson for LIFE. 26,27 —Department of Watershed Management, The University of Arizona, Tucson. 28,29 —Robert Walch. 30,31—George Warmoth Jr. from FPG. 32 through 47—Courtesy Annette E. Carmean and Jean M. F. Dubois, except top page 41, courtesy LIFE Picture Collection, and top page 42, drawing adapted by Nicholas Fasciano from original map courtesy Annette E. Carmean and Jean M. F. Dubois. 50 through 53—Courtesy of The American Museum of Natural History. 59 through 61—Henry de Lumley. 62—Henry de Lumley —drawing courtesy Henry de Lumley. 63 —Henry de Lumley. 64,65—Courtesy Henry de Lumley, drawn by Henri Puech. 66 through 85—Drawings by Harvey Dinnerstein, except pages 74,75, drawings by Burt Silverman. 87—Diagram by Nicholas Fasciano. 88 through 95—Models by Nicholas Fasciano, photographs by Richard Steinberg. 96—George Haling courtesy Professors Ray Dougherty and Michael Helke. 100,101 —Drawings adapted by Nicholas Fasciano. Top row courtesy Spaarnestad Publishing Firm, Haarlem, Holland. Bottom rows courtesy Dr. Irven DeVore, Harvard University. 103—Drawings by Nicholas Fasciano based on research by Philip Lieberman and Edmund S. Crelin. 105—Drawings by Nicholas Fasciano courtesy Saran Jonas. 106—Haskins Laboratories—Voiceprint Laboratories Corporation. 111 through 123—Maps by Nicholas Fasciano, photographs are listed separately: 112—Gordon DeLisle from Alpha Photo Associates. 113—C. L. Gittens from FPG. 114, 115—Andreas Feininger for LIFE. 116—W. King from FPG. 117—Dr. Georg Gerster from Rapho Guillumette. 118,119—J. Ciganovic from Alpha Photo Associates. 120,121—Ed Cooper. 122,123—Victor Englebert from De Wys, Inc. 124—Drawings by Nicholas Fasciano. 132,133—Drawings by Nicholas Fasciano. 137—John Nance from Magnum. 138 through 145—John Launois from Black Star. 146,147—Dolf Herras from Nancy Palmer Photo Agency.

Acknowledgments

Some of the material in Chapter Two is based on an unpublished manuscript, *Trinil, a Biography of Professor Dr. Eugène Dubois, the discoverer of Pithecanthropus erectus,* by Dubois' son, Jean M. F. Dubois, and kindly lent to TIME-LIFE BOOKS by Annette E. Carmean and Jean M. F. Dubois, the grandchildren of the famous discoverer of the first true human.

For the help given in the preparation of this book, the editors are indebted to K. C. Chang, Chairman, Department of Anthropology, Yale University; Edmund S. Crelin, Professor of Anatomy and Human Development, Yale University School of Medicine; Garniss H. Curtis, Professor of Geology, University of California at Berkeley; Henry de Lumley, Director of Research at the National Center of Scientific Research, Marseille; Irven DeVore, Professor of Anthropology, Harvard University; Rhodes W. Fairbridge, Professor of Geology, Columbia University; Leslie G. Freeman Jr., Associate Professor of Anthropology, University of Chicago; Norman Geschwind, James Jackson Putnam Professor of Neurology at Harvard University Medical School; F. Clark Howell, Professor of Anthropology, University of California, Berkeley; Glynn Ll. Isaac, Associate Professor of Anthropology, University of California at Berkeley; Clifford H. Jolly, Associate Professor of Anthropology, New York University; Saran Jonas, New York University Medical Center; Richard B. Lee, Associate Professor of Anthropology, University of Toronto; Philip Lieberman, Professor of Linguistics, University of Connecticut; Alan Mann, Assistant Professor of Anthropology, University of Pennsylvania; William Montagna, Professor of Dermatology at the University of Oregon Medical School; Ian Tattersall, Assistant Curator of Physical Anthropology, Department of Anthropology, American Museum of Natural History; Robert L. Trivers, Harvard University.

Bibliography

General

Butzer, Karl W., *Environment and Archeology*. Aldine, 1964.

Campbell, Bernard G.:
"Conceptual Progress in Physical Anthropology: Fossil Man." *Annual Review of Anthropology, Volume I, 1972*. Annual Reviews, Inc., 1972.
Human Evolution. Aldine, 1966.
ed., *Sexual Selection and the Descent of Man, 1871-1971*. Aldine, 1972.

Count, Earl W., "The Biological Basis of Human Sociality." *American Anthropologist*, Vol. 60, No. 6, 1958.

DeVore, Irven, ed., *Primate Behavior*. Holt, Rinehart and Winston, 1965.

Howells, William W.:
"Homo Erectus." *Scientific American*, Vol. 215, No. 5, 1966.
Mankind in the Making. Doubleday, 1967.

Isaac, Glynn Ll., "The Diet of Early Man: Aspects of Archaeological Evidence from Lower and Middle Pleistocene Sites in Africa." *World Archaeology*, Vol. 2, No. 3, 1971.

Napier, John, *The Roots of Mankind*. Smithsonian Institution Press, 1970.

Pfeiffer, John E., *The Emergence of Man*. Harper and Row, 1969.

Pilbeam, David, *The Ascent of Man*. The Macmillan Co., 1972.

Van Lawick-Goodall, Jane, *In the Shadow of Man*. Houghton-Mifflin, 1971.

Von Koenigswald, G. H. R., *Meeting Prehistoric Man*. Harper and Brothers, 1956.

Washburn, Sherwood L.:
Social Life of Early Man. Aldine, 1961.
and Phyllis Dolhinow, eds., *Perspectives on Human Evolution*, Vol. 2. Holt, Rinehart and Winston, 1972.

Young, J. Z., *An Introduction to the Study of Man*. Oxford University Press, 1971.

Anatomy

Day, Michael H., *Guide to Fossil Man*. World, 1965.

Ju-kang, Woo, "The Skull of Lantian Man." *Current Anthropology*, Vol. 7, No. 1, 1966.

Montagna, William, "The Skin." *Scientific American*, Vol. 212, No. 2, 1965.

Napier, John, "The Evolution of the Hand." *Scientific American*, Vol. 207, No. 6, 1962.

Tobias, Phillip V., *The Brain in Hominid Evolution*. Columbia University Press, 1971.

Communication

Campbell, Bernard G., "The Roots of Language." *Biological and Social Factors in Psycholinguistics*, John Morton, ed., University of Illinois Press, 1970.

Gardner, R. Allen and Beatrice T., "Teaching Sign Language to a Chimpanzee." *Science*, Vol. 165, No. 3894, 1969.

Geschwind, Norman, "The Neural Basis of Language." *Research in Verbal Behavior and Some Neurophysiological Implications*. K. and S. Salzinger, eds., Academic Press, 1967.

Hockett, Charles F., "The Origin of Speech." *Scientific American*, Vol. 203, No. 3, 1960.

Jespersen, Otto, *Language: Its Nature, Development and Origin*. W. W. Norton and Co., 1964.

Lancaster, Jane B., "Primate Communication Systems and the Emergence of Human Language." *Primates: Studies in Adaptation and Variability*, Phyllis C. Jay, ed., Holt, Rinehart and Winston, 1968.

Lieberman, Philip, Edmund S. Crelin and Dennis H. Klatt, "Phonetic Ability and Related Anatomy of the Newborn and Adult Human, Neanderthal Man, and the Chimpanzee." *American Anthropologist*, Vol. 74, No. 3, 1972.

Struhsaker, Thomas T., "Auditory Communication among Vervet Monkeys (Cercopithecus aethiops)." *Social Communication among Primates*, Stuart A. Altmann, ed., University of Chicago Press, 1967.

Hunting

Cloudsley-Thompson, J. L., *Animal Twilight: Man and Game in Eastern Africa*. The Whitefriars Press, 1967.

Coon, Carleton S., *The Hunting Peoples*. Little, Brown and Co., 1971.

Krantz, Grover S., "Brain Size and Hunting Ability in Earliest Man." *Current Anthropology*, Vol. 9, No. 5, 1966.

Kurtén, Björn, *Pleistocene Mammals of Europe*. Aldine, 1968.

Lee, Richard B., and Irven DeVore, eds., *Man the Hunter*. Aldine, 1968.

Service, Elman R., *The Hunters*. Prentice-Hall, 1966.

Vayda, Andrew P., ed., *Environment and Cultural Behavior*. The Natural History Press, 1969.

Sites

Butzer, Karl W., "Acheulian Occupation Sites at Torralba and Ambrona, Spain: Their Geology." *Science*, Vol. 150, No. 3704, 1965.

Chang, Kwang-chih:
The Archaeology of Ancient China. Yale University Press, 1968.
"New Evidence on Fossil Man in China." *Science*, Vol. 136, No. 3518, 1962.

Clark, J. Desmond, *The Prehistory of Africa*. Praeger, 1970.

Cole, Sonia, "A Spanish Camp of Stone Age Elephant Hunters." *New Scientist*, No. 309, 1962.

De Lumley, Henry, "A Paleolithic Camp at Nice." *Scientific American*, Vol. 220, No. 5, 1969.

Hood, Dora, *Davidson Black: a Biography*. University of Toronto Press, 1971.

Howell, F. Clark, "Observations on the Earlier Phases of the European Lower Paleolithic." *American Anthropologist*, Vol. 68, No. 2, 1966.

Isaac, Glynn Ll., "Studies of Early Culture in East Africa." *World Archaeology*, Vol. 1, No. 1, 1969.

Shapiro, Harry L., "The Strange Unfinished Saga of Peking Man." *Natural History*, Vol. LXXX, No. 9, 1971.

Tê-K'un, Chêng:
Archaeology in China, Volume 1: Prehistoric China. Cambridge University Press, 1959.
Archaeology in China, Supplement to Volume 1: New Light on Prehistoric China. Cambridge University Press, 1966.

Tools

Bordaz, Jacques, *Tools of the Old and New Stone Age*. The Natural History Press, 1970.

Oakley, Kenneth P., *Man the Tool-Maker*. Trustees of the British Museum (Natural History), 1961.

Semenov, S. A., *Prehistoric Technology*. Cory, Adams and Mackay, 1964.

Washburn, Sherwood L., "Tools and Human Evolution." *Scientific American*, Vol. 203, No. 3, 1960.

Index

Numerals in italics indicate an illustration of the subject mentioned.

Printed in U.S.A. ⊠